Science Olympiad

Science Olympiad

Highly useful for all school students participating in various Olympiads & Competitions

Series Editor Keshav Mohan

Author Shahana Ansari

Class 2

ARIHANT PRAKASHAN, MEERUT

ARIHANT PRAKASHAN, MEERUT

卐 Administrative & Production Offices

Corporate Office 'Ramchhaya' 4577/15, Agarwal Road, Darya Ganj New Delhi -110002
Tele: 011- 47630600, 43518550; Fax: 011- 23280316

Head Office Kalindi, TP Nagar, Meerut (UP) - 250002
Tele: 0121-2401479, 2512970, 4004199; Fax: 0121-2401648

All disputes subject to Meerut (UP) jurisdiction only.

卐 Sales & Support Offices

Agra, Ahmedabad, Bengaluru, Bhubaneswar, Bareilly, Chennai, Delhi, Guwahati, Haldwani, Hyderabad, Jaipur, Jalandhar, Jhansi, Kolkata, Kota, Lucknow, Meerut, Nagpur & Pune

卐 ISBN 978-93-5251-205-8

卐 Price ₹50

Typeset by Arihant DTP Unit at Meerut
Printed & Bound by Arihant Publications (I) Ltd. (Press Unit)

Production Team

Publishing Manager	Mahendra Singh Rawat	*Cover Designer*	Syed Darin Zaidi
Project Head	Mona Yadav	*Inner Designer*	Deepak Kumar
Project Coordinator	Shahid Saifi	*Page Layouting*	Krishna Kumar Saini
Proof Reader	Mamta Sharma	*DTP Operator*	Mamchand Saini

For further information about the products from Arihant
log on to www.arihantbooks.com or email to info@arihantbooks.com

Preface

Science Olympiad Series for Class 2nd-10th is a series of books which will challenge the young inquisitive minds by the non-routine and exciting problems based on concept of Science.

The main purpose of this series is to make the students ready for competitive exams. The school/board exams are of qualifying nature but not competitive, they do not help the students to prepare for competitive exams, which mainly have objective questions.

- **Need of Olympiad Series**
  This series will fill this gap between the School/Board and Competitive exams as this series have all questions in objective format. This series helps students who are willing to sharpen their problem solving skills. Unlike typical assessment books, which emphasis on drilling practice, the focus of this series is on practicing problem solving techniques.
- **Development of Logical Approach**
  The thought provoking questions given in this series will help students to attain a deeper understanding of the concepts and through which students will be able to impart Reasoning/Logical/Analytical skills in themselves.
- **Complement Your School Studies**
  This series complements the additional preparation needs of students for regular school/board exams. Along with, it will also address all the requirements of the students who are approaching National/State level Olympiads.

I shall welcome criticism from the students, teachers, educators and parents. I would also like to hear from all of you about errors and deficiencies, which may have remained in this edition and the suggestions for the next edition.

Editor

CONTENTS

Living and Non-Living Things

1. Which of these characteristics is shown by both living and non-living things?

(a) Growth (b) Reproduction
(c) Breathing (d) Weight

2. Which of the following is a natural non-living thing?

(a)  (b) 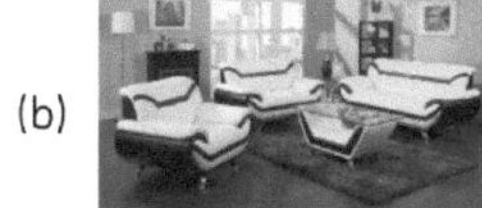

(c)  (d) 

3. Match the things shown in the pictures with the tastes given below :

A.  (i) Sour

B.  (ii) Bitter

C.  (iii) Sweet

D.  (iv) Salty

Codes

	A	B	C	D
(a)	(iii)	(ii)	(i)	(iv)
(b)	(i)	(ii)	(iii)	(iv)
(c)	(iv)	(iii)	(i)	(ii)
(d)	(iv)	(iii)	(ii)	(i)

4. Which of the following is a living thing?

(a) 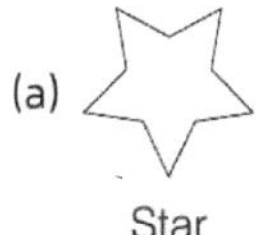
Star

(b) 
Moon

(c) 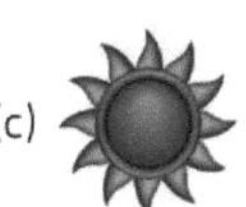
Sun

(d) 
Herb

5. Complete the following web chart.

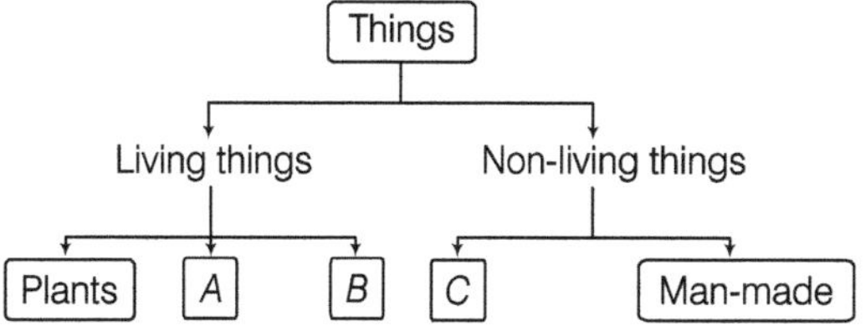

	A	B	C
(a)	Trees	Herbs	Rivers
(b)	Plants	Trees	Mountains
(c)	Animals	Human beings	Natural
(d)	Trees	Animals	Rivers

6. Which of these is a correct option?
(a) Living and non-living things are made up of same material
(b) Living and non-living things occupy space
(c) Living and non-living things have weight
(d) Both (b) and (c)

7. Look at the pictures. The fruits which are eaten by us.

A. 
Guava

B. 
Mango

C.  
Apple

D. 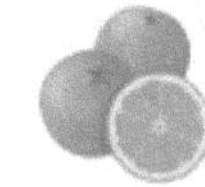
Orange

Reeta while eating these fruits asks her mother that tell her the state of these fruits. Whether they are living or non-living?

Her mother told her that they are
(a) living (b) non-living
(c) Both (a) and (b) (d) Neither (a) nor (b)

8. A cockroach feels changes with the help of
(a) nose
(b) wings
(c) antenna
(d) eyes

9. The given picture shown in a garden.

(a) Only children are living beings
(b) Children and swings are living beings
(c) Bicycle and swings are living things as they move
(d) Children, plants, animals and birds are living beings

10. Look at this picture.

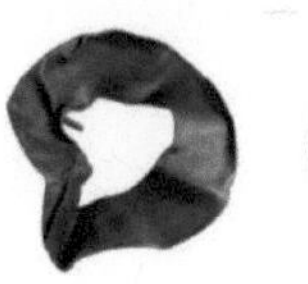 

When we pump air in a tyre tube, the tube becomes bigger and rounder, it shows that tube
(a) is non-living (b) is living
(c) has grown (d) None of these

11. All living things feel changes around them. Plants grow towards the light. It shows that plant also ..*A*.. but plants do not have ..*B*...
(a) *A*– move, *B*–legs
(b) *A*– bend, *B*–skin
(c) *A*– feel, *B*–sense organs
(d) *A*– move, *B*–shape

Plants grow towards light

12. Look at the picture carefully and choose the correct option.

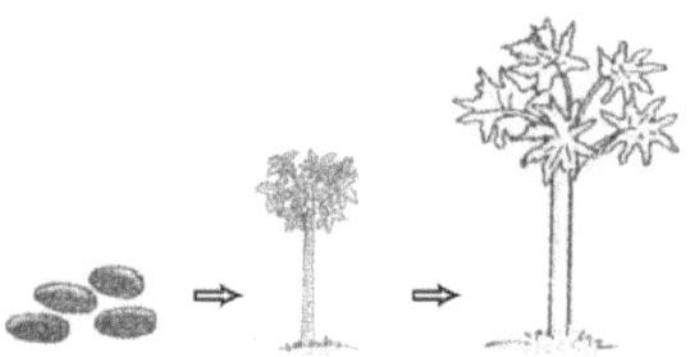

A seed is a living thing because
(a) it grows into a plant (b) it does not breathe
(c) it does not move (d) it does not grows

13. Plants like touch me not is a living thing because it

(a) breathes
(b) grow
(c) shows movement upon touching
(d) All of the above

14. We are surrounded by many living things and non-living things. So, classify them as living or non-living.

A. Milk B. Tree

C. Men

D. Cooking oil

Codes

	A	B	C	D
(a)	Living	Non-living	Non-living	Living
(b)	Non-living	Living	Non-living	Non-living
(c)	Non-living	Living	Living	Non-living
(d)	Living	Non-living	Living	Non-living

15. Living things need air to breathe.

Which structure is used by the following organisms to breathe?

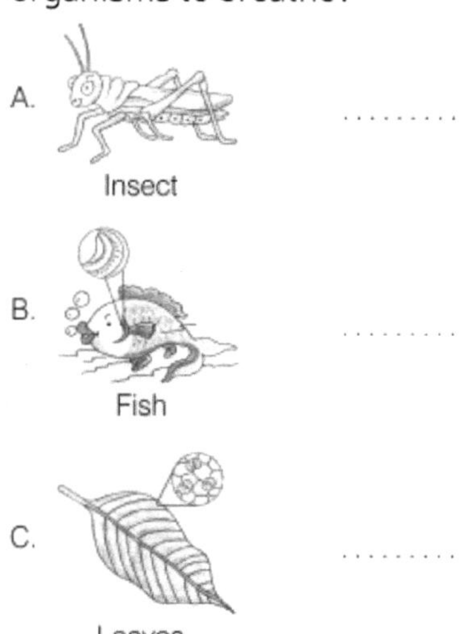

A. Insect ....

B. Fish ....

C. Leaves ....

Codes

	A	B	C
(a)	Wings	Lungs	Leaves
(b)	Legs	Lungs	Pores
(c)	Air holes	Gills	Stomata
(d)	Stomach	Gills	Stomata

16. Which one of the following refers to non-living things?

(a) Fan, kite, bird
(b) Table, chair, child
(c) Clouds, rivers, mountains
(d) Rivers, birds, trees

17. The given figure shows a black box containing an object. Kunal put his hand into the box and made the following comments.

It is cold.

It is rough.

It is hard.

Which sense organ is involved for Kunal to make these descriptions?

(a) Ear (b) Tongue (c) Skin (d) Nose

18. On Earth, all the things are characterised into two categories as living thing and non-living things. Some statements are given below about non-living things state which among them are correct.

(a) Non-living things do not need food, air and water
(b) Non-living things do not breathe
(c) Non-living things do not reproduce
(d) All of the above

19. The picture shows the parent with their young ones. What quality is depicted by them?

(a) Move (b) Grow
(c) Need food (d) Reproduce

20. A butterfly with some flowers is placed in a glass jar and tightly closed with a lid. A butterfly died because there is no .... in the glass jar.

(a) air (b) water (c) light (d) food

Plants

1. The leaves of a neem tree are used as

(a) spices (b) paper
(c) medicine (d) rubber

2. Which of the following plant is a herb?

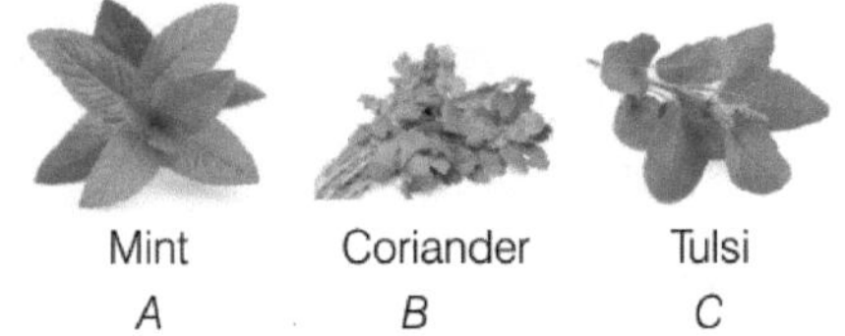

(a) Only *A* (b) Only *B*
(c) Only *C* (d) All of these

3. Write the name and type of the following plant.

(a) Pumpkin, climber (b) Pumpkin, creeper
(c) Watermelon, climber (d) Watermelon, creeper

4. Some trees are very different from others. Why banyan tree is different from other trees?

Banyan tree

(a) It is a tall tree
(b) Banyan tree has no branches
(c) Banyan trees have roots growing from their branches
(d) Trunks of banyan tree are whitish

5. In which of the following plants stem is eaten by us?

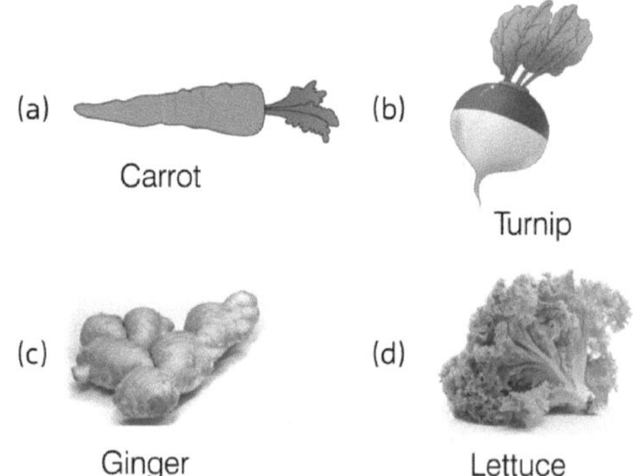

6. Match the following columns.

	Column I		Column II
A.	*Hydrilla*	(i)	Herb
B.	Rose plant	(ii)	Shrub
C.	Mint	(iii)	Water plant

Codes

	A	B	C
(a)	(iii)	(ii)	(i)
(b)	(i)	(ii)	(iii)
(c)	(i)	(iii)	(ii)
(d)	(ii)	(iii)	(i)

7. Plants can make their own food. The process of making food by the plants is known as

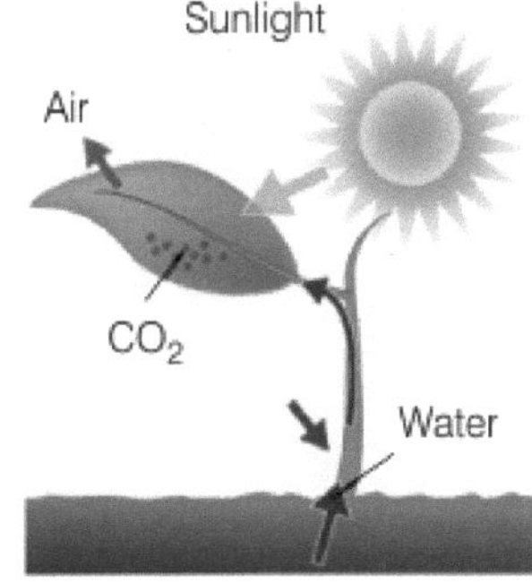

(a) germination
(b) factory
(c) photosynthesis
(d) breathing

8. Which natural fibre is obtained from this plant?

(a) Cotton
(b) Jute
(c) Wool
(d) Leather

9. Match the following columns.

	Column I		Column II
A.	Bamboos	(i)	To make medicine
B.	Tulsi	(ii)	To make sugar
C.	Jasmine	(iii)	To make furniture
D.	Sugarcane	(iv)	To make perfumes

Codes

	A	B	C	D
(a)	(ii)	(i)	(iii)	(iv)
(b)	(iii)	(i)	(iv)	(ii)
(c)	(i)	(iii)	(iv)	(ii)
(d)	(i)	(ii)	(iv)	(iii)

10. Which of the following part prepares food for the plant?

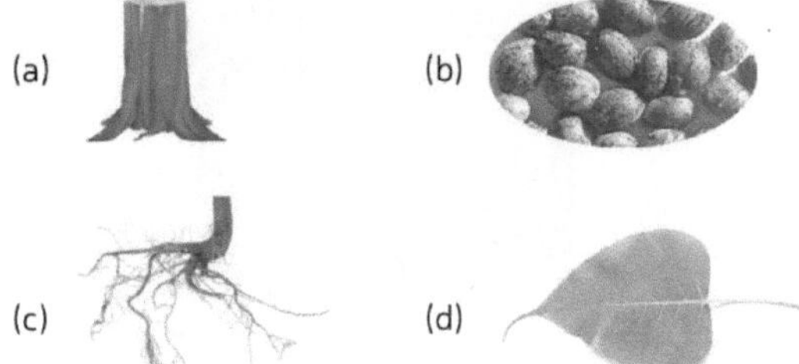

(a) (b) (c) (d)

11. Guess my name.

I easily grow in desert area.
I have thorns.
I can store water in my stem.
Who am I?

(a) Rose (b) *Canna* (c) *Cactus* (d) *Hibiscus*

12. In sugarcane plants, the extra food is stored in the

Sugarcane

(a) roots (b) leaves
(c) stem (d) branches

13. Two climber plants that have weak and soft stem are

(a) money plant, rose
(b) merigold, rose
(c) pea plant, bean plant
(d) grapevine, money plant

14. Complete the sentence, by filling the correct option.

To make food, a plant uses air, water and the ......*A*...... and this process is called ......*B*...... .

(a) *A*–leaves, *B*–germination
(b) *A*–sunlight, *B*–photosynthesis
(c) *A*–soil, *B*–plant
(d) *A*–oxygen, *B*–breathing

15. Fill the correct options in the given blanks.

I. Plant grows from................ .
II. The fruit grows from the ....
III. Buds grow on the ....

Codes

	I	II	III
(a)	roots	seed	leaves
(b)	roots	seed	stem
(c)	seed	flower	stem
(d)	seed	leaves	branches

16. Look at the figure and answer the question.

A palm is a .....*A*......... tree and palm trees have no ....*B*....... .

	A	*B*
(a)	big,	leaves
(b)	small,	flowers
(c)	big,	fruits
(d)	tall,	branches

17. Which part we eat in the wheat plant?

(a) Leaves
(b) Roots
(c) Grains
(d) All of these

18. Which part of the plant absorb water and minerals for the growth of plant?

(a) Leaves
(b) Stem
(c) Branches
(d) Root

19. Which part of the plant fixes it firmly in the soil?

Rose

Hibiscus

(a) Root
(b) Stem
(c) Branches
(d) None of the above

20. Which of the following plant is creeper?

A

B

C

D

(a) Only *A*
(b) Only *B*
(c) Only *C*
(d) Only *D*

21. Look at the pictures and tell which of the following statements are correct?

I

II

I. Plants make the air clean and fresh.
II. Plants give shadows.

Codes

(a) Only I is correct
(b) Only II is incorrect
(c) I and II are correct
(d) I and II are not correct

22. The following plants are examples of

Money plant

Grapevine

(a) creepers
(b) climbers
(c) shrubs
(d) herbs

23. Which of these is incorrectly matched?

	Part we eat	Plant part
(a)		Root
(b)		Flower
(c)		Leaves
(d)		Fruit

Animals

1. Which of the following animals give milk to us?

(a)  (b) 

(c)  (d) All of these

2. Which of the following animal is a pet animal?

(a) Rat (b) Polar bear

(c) 
Dog

(d) 
Squirrel

3. A colt is a baby of

(a) 
Dog

(b) 
Horse

(c) 
Goat

(d) 
Cow

4. Domestic animals need shelters for

(a) help them grow (b) protection
(c) get food and water (d) stay alive

5. The following animals are

Rat

Wolf

Pigs

Bear

(a) carnivores
(b) herbivores
(c) omnivores
(d) All of the above

6. Which one of the following is carnivores?

(a) 

(b) 

(c) 

(d) 

7. Match the animals with their food.

	Column I		Column II
A.		(i)	
B.		(ii)	
C.		(iii)	
D.		(iv)	

Codes

	A	B	C	D		A	B	C	D
(a)	(ii)	(iii)	(iv)	(i)	(b)	(iii)	(iv)	(ii)	(i)
(c)	(iii)	(ii)	(i)	(iv)	(d)	(ii)	(iv)	(iii)	(i)

8. The animals which need for transportation and for field work are known as

Oxen ploughing field

Elephant carrying logs

(a) dairy animals
(b) wild animals
(c) aquatic animals
(d) draught animals

9. The animal which carry their young one in a pouch and is found in Australia is
(a) panda
(b) polar bear
(c) kangaroo
(d) penguin

10. Match the animals with their homes.

	Column I		Column II
A.	Dog	(i)	Shed
B.	Horse	(ii)	Den
C.	Lion	(iii)	Kennel
D.	Cow	(iv)	Stable

Codes

	A	B	C	D
(a)	(iii)	(iv)	(ii)	(i)
(b)	(iv)	(iii)	(ii)	(i)
(c)	(i)	(iii)	(ii)	(iv)
(d)	(ii)	(iv)	(iii)	(i)

11. Which of these animals provides us wool?

(a) 
Sheep

(b) Goat

(c) 
Yak

(d) All of these

12. .... make honey from the juice of flowers.

(a) Butterfly
(b) Silkworm
(c) Flies
(d) Bees

13. A zebra's young one is called a

(a) cub
(b) colt
(c) kid
(d) lamb

14. Look at the following figures *A* and *B*.

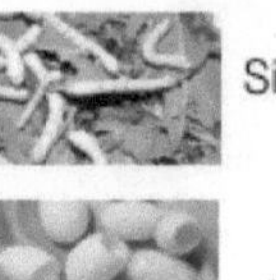
Silkworms

Cocoons

A *B*

These animals provide us
(a) milk and egg
(b) fur and egg
(c) wool and silk thread
(d) milk and silk thread

15. Which one of the following animals does not help to carry loads?

(a) Bullock (b) Camel
(c) Donkey (d) Dog

16. Write the name of the given bird and the food it like to eat, choose the correct options.

(a) Eagle, insects
(b) Vulture, small animals ,meat
(c) Swallows, grains
(d) Woodpecker, insects

17. Match the birds with their sounds.

	Column I		Column II
A.	Owl	(i)	Chirp-chirp
B.	Koel	(ii)	Caw-caw

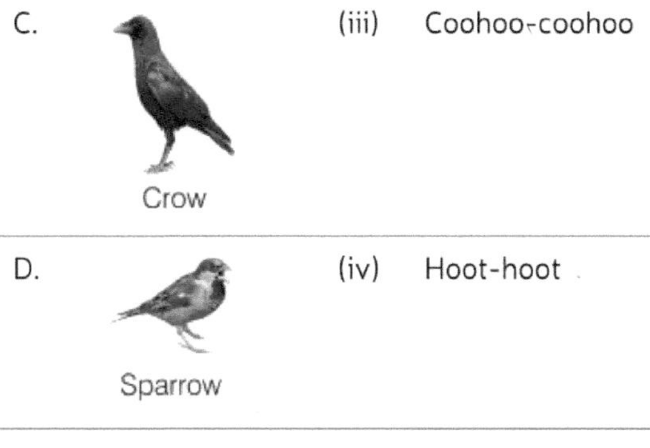

C.	Crow	(iii)	Coohoo-coohoo
D.	Sparrow	(iv)	Hoot-hoot

Codes

	A	B	C	D
(a)	(ii)	(iii)	(iv)	(i)
(b)	(iv)	(iii)	(ii)	(i)
(c)	(iii)	(ii)	(iv)	(i)
(d)	(i)	(ii)	(iii)	(iv)

18. Guess my name.

I eat vegetables and bones.
I live in kennel.
I guard your home.
I says bow-bow.
Who am I?

(a) Cat (b) Dog
(c) Rabbit (d) Cow

19. Guess my name.

I have six legs.
I have two antennae also.
Who am I?

(a) A mosquito (b) A housefly
(c) A cockroach (d) A spider

20. Give two examples of animals, who eat only plants.

(a) Cow, goat (b) Cow, tiger
(c) Deer, frog (d) Dolphin, rabbit

21. Tortoises are protected from enemies due to

Tortoises

(a) thick legs (b) long neck
(c) thick shell (d) large mouth

22. Which of the following group shows aquatic animals?

23. Leather is used to make bags, shoes, purses, belts, wallets, jackets and so on. It is made from the .... of animals.

(a) teeth
(b) wool
(c) skin
(d) dung

24. Mark 🙂, if true and 🙁, if false.

I. Dairy animals gives us meat.
II. Carrot is the favourite food of rabbit.
III. Eggs lays by hen are rich in proteins.

Codes

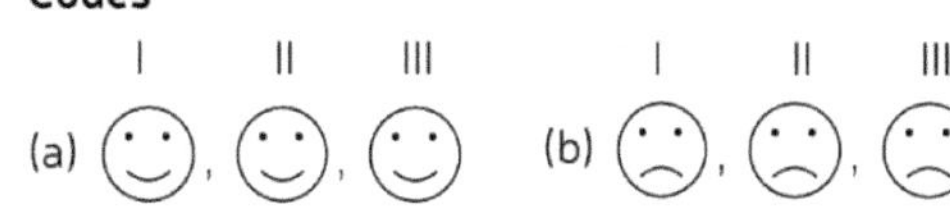

25. Which of these birds has a beak that helps it to suck nectar from the flower?

(a) Humming bird (b) Eagle
(c) Pigeon (d) Goose

26. A group of elephants is called a

Elephant

(a) mob
(b) school
(c) parade
(d) colony

27. Match the following breathing organs with the animals they belong to

	Column I		Column II
A.	Lungs	(i)	*Amoeba*
B.	Gills	(ii)	Humans
C.	Body surface	(iii)	Insects
D.	Spiracles	(iv)	Fishes

Codes

	A	B	C	D
(a)	(iv)	(i)	(ii)	(iii)
(b)	(iii)	(i)	(iv)	(ii)
(c)	(ii)	(iv)	(i)	(iii)
(d)	(iii)	(i)	(ii)	(iv)

28. There are some domestic animals names are hidden in this word puzzle. Find them and answer the question that follows.

M	L	T	U	J	K	O	C	O	W
B	F	B	U	F	F	A	L	O	X
U	N	I	M	F	O	N	D	W	E
F	I	H	G	O	A	T	R	S	T
I	A	R	P	G	N	C	O	X	K
T	S	Q	B	T	L	U	M	J	Y

How many words are there in the box?

(a) 7 (b) 4
(c) 8 (d) 6

Human Body

1. Ramu while preparing tea got a burn. Which sense organ tell him the sense of hotness.

(a) Eyes
(b) Ears
(c) Skin
(d) Both (a) and (c)

2. Which of the following organ is used in breathing?

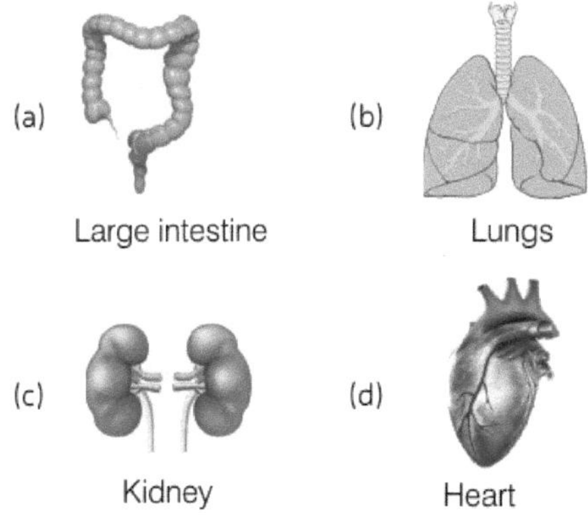

3. Which of the following organ control all our actions like seeing, hearing, walking and learning?

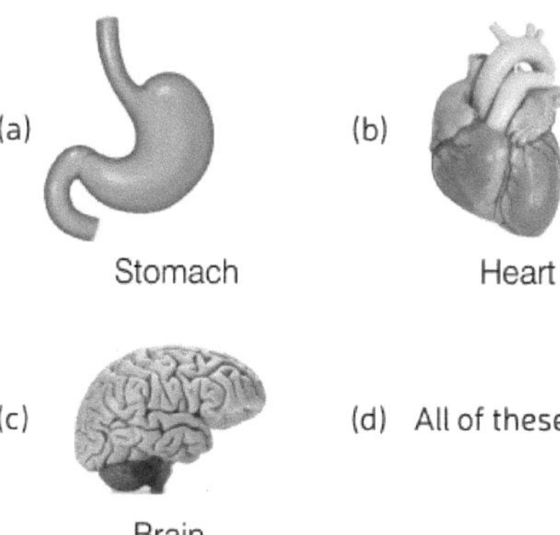

4. Which of the following sense organ can feel cold temperature ?

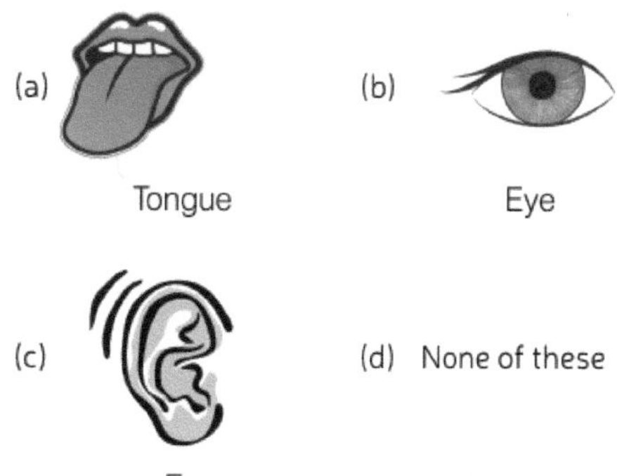

5. Match the sense organs with their function.

Column I	Column II
A.	(i)
B.	(ii)
C.	(iii)
D.	(iv)

Codes

	A	B	C	D		A	B	C	D
(a)	(iv)	(iii)	(i)	(ii)	(b)	(i)	(ii)	(iii)	(iv)
(c)	(iii)	(iv)	(ii)	(i)	(d)	(iii)	(iv)	(i)	(ii)

6. The given organ is protected in

(a) skull
(b) heart
(c) kidney
(d) small intestine

7. Which sense organ help us to taste?

(a) Nose
(b) Skin
(c) Tongue
(d) Eyes

8. Which of the following part is paired in our body?

(a) Eyes
(b) Ears
(c) Legs
(d) All of these

9. The given system represents the

(a) circulatory system
(b) respiratory system
(c) digestive system
(d) excretory system

10. Label the parts *A* and *B* in the given diagram of skeletal system.

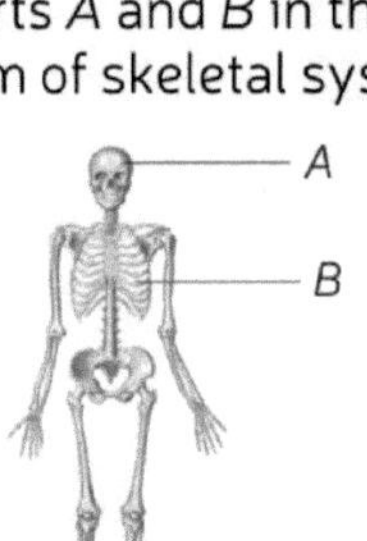

Skeletal system

	A	*B*
(a)	Brain	Chest
(b)	Brain	Heart
(c)	Skull	Ribs
(d)	Nerves	Ribs

11. How many bones are there in our body?

(a) 200 bones
(b) 210 bones
(c) 206 bones
(d) 300 bones

12. Complete the following sentence.

The main function of respiratory system is to take ...... *A* ...... and give out ...... *B* ...... and the process is known as ...... *C* ....

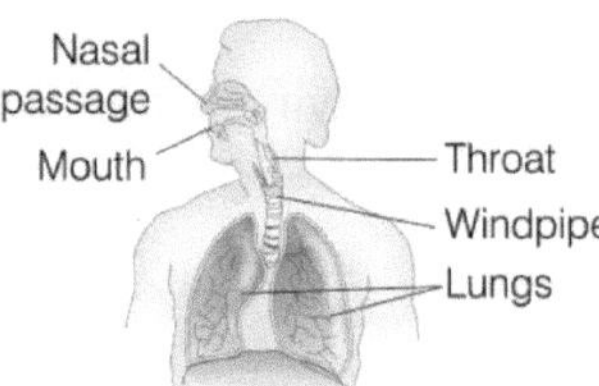

Respiratory system

	A	*B*	*C*
(a)	carbon dioxide	oxygen	digestion
(b)	oxygen	carbon dioxide	digestion
(c)	oxygen	carbon dioxide	breathing
(d)	carbon dioxide	oxygen	breating

13. The main function of heart is

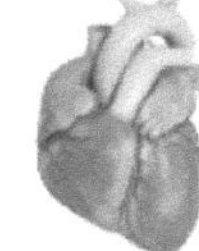
Heart

(a) to control all organs and body parts
(b) to digest food and give energy
(c) to pump blood in the whole body
(d) to give shape and support to body

14. Write true or false.

I. Food help us to grow.
II. We see with our ears.
III. We feel things with our skin.

Codes

	I	II	III		I	II	III
(a)	T	T	T	(b)	T	F	F
(c)	T	F	T	(d)	F	T	T

15. Which part is incorrectly matched?

	Function	Organ
(a)	Pumping of blood	Heart
(b)	Breathing	Ribs
(c)	Digestion of food	Stomach
(d)	Thinking process	Brain

16. Mark the place *A* in the given figure.

The ...... *A* ...... is a place in a human body where two bones meet.

(a) bone
(b) knee
(c) posture
(d) joint

17. Guess my name.
I am the main organ of your body.
I work day and night in your body and do not need rest.
I made up of muscles. Who am I?

(a) Stomach (b) Brain
(c) Heart (d) Kidney

18. Look at the following diagram. The given system shows the

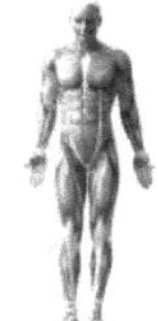

(a) circulatory system (b) muscular system
(c) skeleton system (d) None of these

19. What is the function of the system given below?

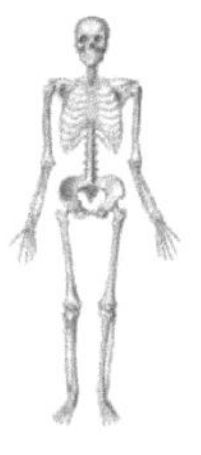
Skeletal system

(a) It control all the activities of body
(b) It helps in breathing
(c) It helps in digesting the food
(d) It gives shape and support to our body

20. Pick the incorrect statement .

(a) The skin helps us to feel things
(b) The eyes help us to make (the difference of) colours and shapes
(c) Muscular system gives shape and support to our body
(d) Our brain is protected by the skull

21. Choose the correct statement.

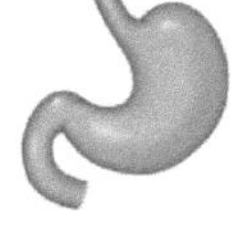

(a) I pump blood to all parts of your body
(b) I clean the blood
(c) I digest the food
(d) I help in taking oxygen

22. Which organ system helps in breathing?

(a) Digestive system
(b) Circulatory system
(c) Respiratory system
(d) Nervous system

23. Look at the figure given below.

Pick the correct statement.

Muscles

(a) Our bones are not covered with muscles
(b) Muscles help to move bones
(c) There are about 300 muscles in our body.
(d) Muscles give support to our body

24. The two organs located in our chest are

(a) stomach, intestine
(b) heart, stomach
(c) heart, lungs
(d) lungs, stomach

25. Name the body part which has all the sense organs present in it.

(a) Stomach (b) Heart
(c) Hands (d) Head

Food and Nutrition

1. Food is necessary for us because
(a) food helps us to grow (b) food gives us energy
(c) food keeps us healthy (d) All options are correct

2. The main sources of our food are
(a) plants (b) animals
(c) Both (a) and (b) (d) None of these

3. The given food items are sources of

Ghee, Butter, Potato, Rice, Wheat

(a) proteins (b) vitamins and minerals
(c) carbohydrates and fats (d) roughage

4. The given food items provide us

Fruits, vegetables and green leaves

(a) proteins (b) carbohydrates
(c) vitamins and minerals (d) fats

5. We get cereals, pulses, vegetables and nuts from

(a) plants (b) animals
(c) Both (a) and (b) (d) None of these

6. Boiled water is better than normal water because boiling kills
(a) microbes (b) soil
(c) nutrients (d) chlorine

7. ....are known as gateways of knowledge.
(a) Sense organs (b) Excretory organ
(c) Hands (d) Blood vessels

8. Which of these foods help us to grow?

Fruits

Bread

Rice

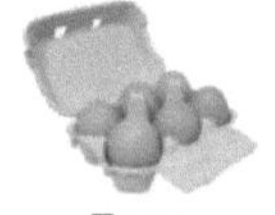

Eggs

Chicken

Milk

(a) Fruits and bread (b) Fruits and rice
(c) Eggs and rice (d) Eggs, chicken and milk

9. The given food items are examples of

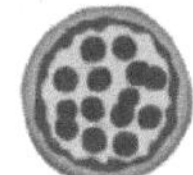
Pizza

Hot dogs

French fries

Popcorn

(a) healthy food (b) junk food
(c) nutritious food (d) protective food

10. Which one is the healthy food?

(a) 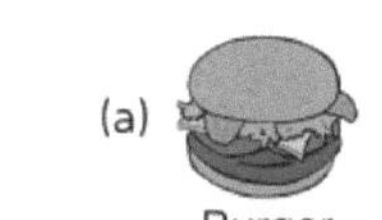
Burger

(b) 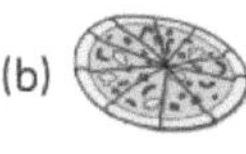
Pizza

(c) 
Chocolates

(d) 
Apple

11. Mark (smiling face), if true and (sad face), if false.

I. Wash fruits and vegetables before eating.
II. Cereals are animals products.
III. All vegetables should be taken as raw.

Codes

I II III I II III

(a)  (b) 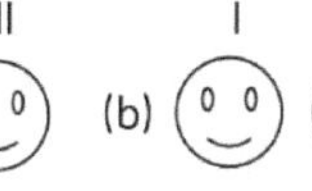 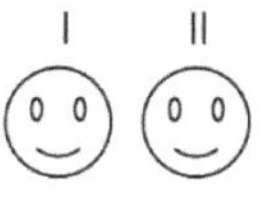 

(c)  (d)  

12. The method of making sprouts from seeds is called sprouting. Sprouting makes the food

Chana

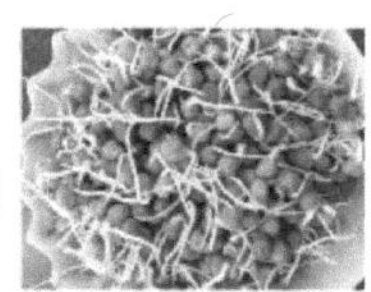
Sprouts

Making of sprouts

(a) tasty (b) healthy
(c) nutritious (d) not edible

13. Which of these are protective food?

(a) 
Apple

(b) 
Papaya

(c) 
Pomegranate

(d) All of these

14. Eating nuts are very healthy because nuts gives us lot of

Almonds

Walnuts

Pistachios

(a) vitamins (b) minerals
(c) roughage (d) energy

15. People who eat fish, meat and chicken are called

(a) vegetarian (b) non-vegetarian
(c) carnivorous (d) omnivorous

16. Which of the following pair is incorrectly matched?

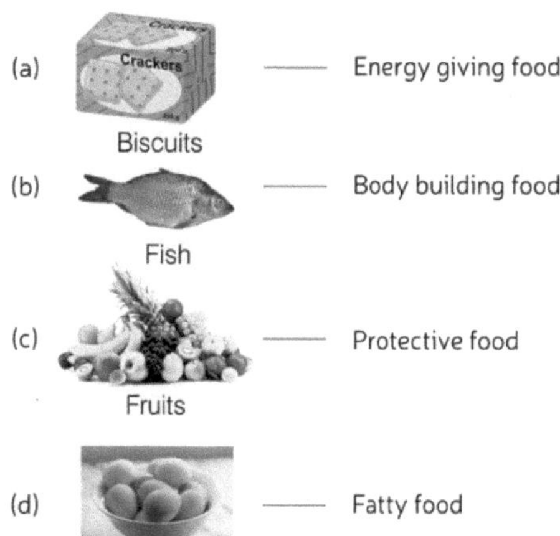

17. Which statement is not correct for minerals?

(a) They can be taken from plants and animals
(b) They give energy
(c) They are not destroyed during food preparation
(d) They help in maintaining water balance in the body

18. Match the following columns .

	Column I	Column II
A.	Milk	(i) Protein
B.	Dal and roti	(ii) Junk food
C.	Eggs	(iii) Calcium
D.	Cold drinks	(iv) Carbohydrate

Codes

	A	B	C	D
(a)	(iv)	(iii)	(ii)	(i)
(b)	(iii)	(iv)	(i)	(ii)
(c)	(iii)	(iv)	(ii)	(i)
(d)	(iv)	(iii)	(i)	(ii)

19. Which of these are good habits?

(a) Wash your hands after you use the toilet
(b) Keep your nails trimmed and clean
(c) Brush your teeth twice a day
(d) All of the above

20. It helps in the chewing of food and cause the first digestion of food.

(a) Teeth (b) Mouth
(c) Stomach (d) Kidney

21. Mummy says us to eat green vegetables like spinach because they are

(a) protective foods
(b) body building foods
(c) energy giving foods
(d) None of these

22. Milk is called a complete food because

Milk

(a) it helps us to grow
(b) it protects us from falling sick
(c) it gives us energy to work and play
(d) All of the above

23. Among the given food items, write the items which are obtained from plants .

(a) Bread, tomato soup, omelette
(b) Bread, tomato soup, milk
(c) Chick peas, milk
(d) Chick peas, tomato soup , bread

24. Choose the correct statement.

(a) Milk is called a complete food
(b) A vegetarian diet includes only fruits, vegetables, pulses and milk
(c) Vitamins and minerals protect us from diseases
(d) All of the above

25. Match the following columns .

	Column I		Column II
A.	Energy giving food	(i)	Fruits and vegetables
B.	Roadside food	(ii)	Spicy fried potatoes
C.	Meals	(iii)	Rice and bread
D.	Healthy food	(iv)	Three in a day
E.	Oily food	(v)	Covered with dust and flies

Codes

	A	B	C	D	E
(a)	(iii)	(v)	(iv)	(i)	(ii)
(b)	(ii)	(i)	(iii)	(v)	(iv)
(c)	(iii)	(v)	(ii)	(i)	(iv)
(d)	(ii)	(iii)	(iv)	(i)	(v)

26. Give one word for each of the following statements I and II.

Statement I Drink plenty of this keeps us healthy ....

Statement II We must use this to throw the waste food ....

	Statement I	Statement II
(a)	juice	roadside
(b)	milk	kitchen
(c)	water	dustbin
(d)	honey	dustbin

27. Look at the picture shown below. Write *E* for energy giving food. *B* for body building food and *P* for protective food.

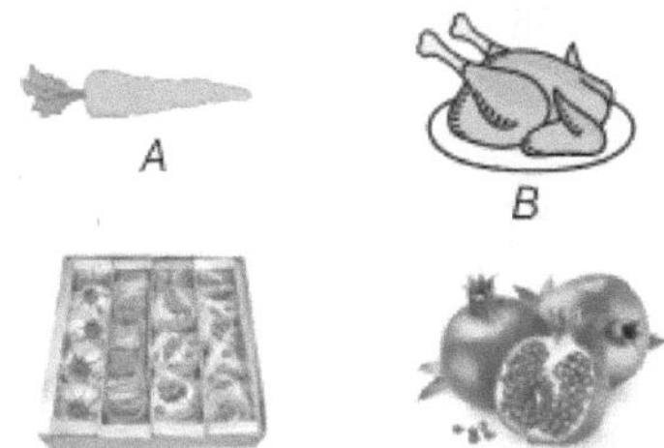

C *D*

Codes

	A	B	C	D		A	B	C	D
(a)	*B*	*E*	*B*	*P*	(b)	*P*	*B*	*E*	*P*
(c)	*B*	*B*	*E*	*P*	(d)	*B*	*P*	*E*	*B*

28. Some food items are eaten raw. They keep our body healthy. If these food items are cooked, then what will happen?

Raw food

(a) They will become poisonous
(b) There protective nutrients may be lost due to heat
(c) They will get spoiled
(d) None of the above

29. Match the following columns.

Column I	Column II
A.	(i) Bath regularly
B.	(ii) Play with sharp objects
C.	(iii) Trim your nails
D.	(iv) Brush your teeth

Codes

	A	B	C	D
(a)	(i)	(ii)	(iii)	(iv)
(b)	(iv)	(ii)	(i)	(iii)
(c)	(ii)	(iii)	(iv)	(i)
(d)	(iv)	(iii)	(ii)	(i)

30. The given diagram shows

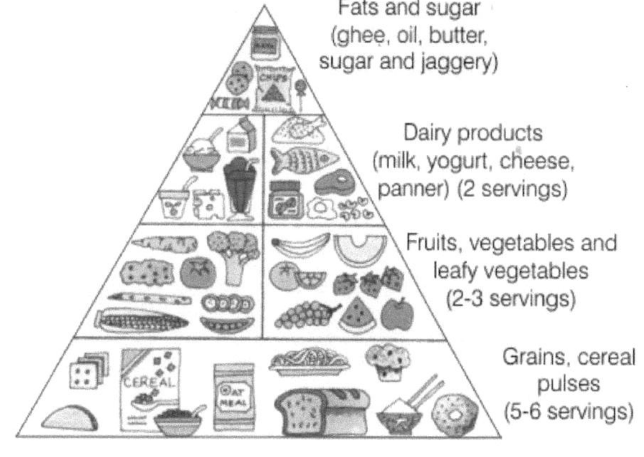

(a) food web
(b) food pyramid
(c) food chain
(d) All of the above

Housing and Clothing

1. Which one of the following is a strong house?

(a)  (b) 

(c) 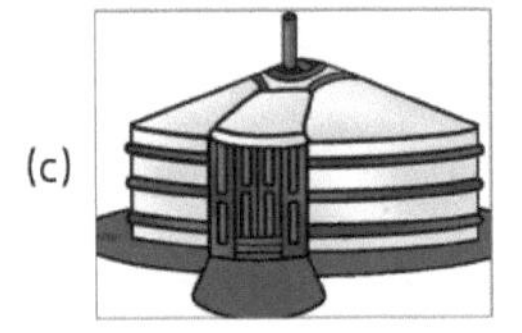 (d) 

2. Soldiers and construction workers live in a

(a)  (b) 

(c)  (d) None of these

3. Some houses are made from blocks of ice. Such houses are called

(a) 

Kutcha house

(b) 
Pucca house

(c) 

Igloo house

(d) Caravan house

4. The following types of clothes protect us from

(a) summer (b) winter

(c) rain (d) All of these

5. Look at the picture carefully and choose the correct option.

(a) They have many homes in one building
(b) Each of them is called a flat
(c) These houses are very strong and are made from bricks, cement and steel
(d) All of the above

6. Match the following columns.

	Column I		Column II
A.		(i)	
B.		(ii)	
C.		(iii)	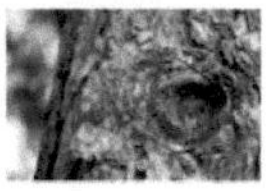
D.		(iv)	
E.		(v)	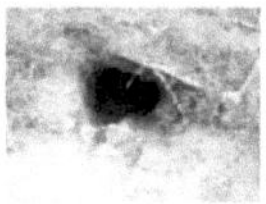

Codes

	A	B	C	D	E
(a)	(iii)	(i)	(v)	(ii)	(iv)
(b)	(ii)	(i)	(iii)	(v)	(iv)
(c)	(iii)	(i)	(ii)	(v)	(iv)
(d)	(iii)	(i)	(v)	(iv)	(ii)

7. Which of the following statements are correct about the house given below?

(a) These houses are raised from the ground level on bamboo stilts
(b) These houses are made in areas, where it rains heavily
(c) This does not let the water or snakes enter the house
(d) All of the above

8. Which of the following statement is incorrect?
(a) Houses in the hills have sloping roofs
(b) A cottage is a small house
(c) All houses are build of mud only
(d) Houses in the plains have flat roof

9. Read the clue and name the house.

A foldable house which are used by nomads.
(a) Caravan (b) A hut
(c) A tent house (d) A cottage

10. Which of the following is not a permanent house?

(a) 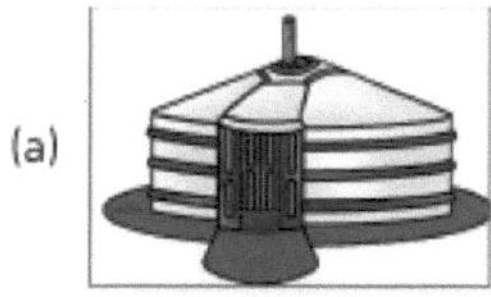 A yurt

(b)  A bungalow

(c)  A cottage

(d)  Apartment

11. We wear cotton and light colour clothes in summer as

(a) they keep our body warm
(b) they absorbs heat
(c) they keep our body cool
(d) do not absorb sweat

12. We share our homes with some unwanted visitors. These animals are not our pet. So, who are they? Take the help of picture.

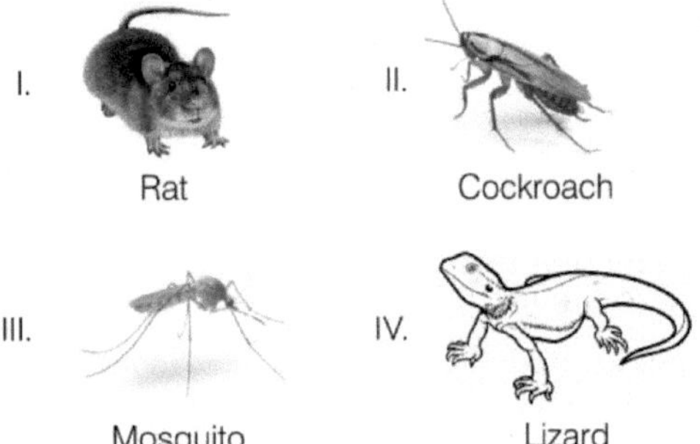

(a) Friends
(b) Pests
(c) Utensils
(d) All of the above

13. Draw ☺, if true and ☹, if false for the given statements.

I. Kutcha houses are strong.
II. A hut is made up of blocks of ice.

Codes

	I	II			I	II
(a)	☺	☺		(b)	☹	☹
(c)	☺	☹		(d)	☹	☺

14. Choose the correct option.
The picture shows

(a) we wear sweaters, gloves, etc., to keep ourselves warm
(b) cold, dry air blows in winter season
(c) we sometimes light fire to keep us warm
(d) All of the above

15. Match the following columns.

	Column I		Column II
A.	A fabric that keeps us cool in summer	(i)	Waterproof
B.	Hair of animals used to make clothes	(ii)	Cotton
C.	A material which does not let water to pass through	(iii)	Wool

Codes

	A	B	C			A	B	C
(a)	(i)	(ii)	(iii)		(b)	(ii)	(iii)	(i)
(c)	(iii)	(ii)	(i)		(d)	(iii)	(i)	(ii)

16. Match the following columns.

	Column I		Column II
A	Cotton plants	(i)	
B	Jute plants	(ii)	
C	Sheep	(iii)	
D	Silkworm	(iv) 	

Codes

	A	B	C	D			A	B	C	D
(a)	(iv)	(i)	(iii)	(ii)		(b)	(iii)	(i)	(iv)	(ii)
(c)	(iii)	(iv)	(i)	(ii)		(d)	(iv)	(i)	(ii)	(iii)

17. People living in house boats move in and out of their houses in

(a) caravans (b) tents
(c) shikaras (d) igloo

18. Which of the following materials is not used to build a kutcha house?

Kutcha house

(a) Bamboo (b) Cement
(c) Straw (d) Grass

19. Nylon ropes are widely available, nylon is

Nylon ropes

(a) a kind of natural cotton
(b) a kind of natural silk
(c) man- made fibre
(d) All of the above

20. Look at the picture carefully and choose the correct option for the pictures.

Mountain goat

Sheep

Mountain camel

(a) We get wool fibres from these animals
(b) Wool is obtained from the skin of these animals
(c) Wool fibres are used to make woollen clothes
(d) All of the above

21. Match the clothes with the season you would wear in.

	Column I (Clothes)	Column II (Seasons)
A.		(i) Summer
B.		(ii) Winter
C.		(iii) Rainy
D.		

Codes

	A	B	C	D
(a)	(ii)	(ii)	(i)	(iii)
(b)	(i)	(ii)	(ii)	(iii)
(c)	(i)	(ii)	(i)	(iii)
(d)	(ii)	(ii)	(iii)	(i)

22. Building walls purposes are to support roofs, floors and ceilings.

The buildings material which is mainly used in constructions of walls is

(a) cement
(b) wood
(c) rubber
(d) plastic

Safety and First Aid

1. If you play with a knife or scissors you might get

(a) burn (b) hurt (c) diseases (d) cut

2. What is pedestrian crossing?
   (a) White and black strips on the road for safe crossing
   (b) It is a place where vehicles can park
   (c) It is a path were pedestrian can walk
   (d) It is a crossing where zebras cross

3. Which one of the following is a traffic inspector?

(a)  

(b) 

(c) 

(d) None of these

4. While riding a bicycle on the road, one should always keep

(a) to the right of the roadside
(b) in the middle of the road
(c) to the North of the road
(d) to the left of the roadside

5. Which of the following safety rules is/are correct, while we go for swimming?

(a) Swim only in the presence of an adult
(b) Use floaters or swimming tubes, if you are learning how to swim
(c) Never go to the deep inside of a pool
(d) All of the above

6. The given picture shows the symbol of

(a) playground (b) hospital
(c) danger (d) jungle

7. Draw ☺, if statement is true and ☹, if statement is false.

I. 

II. 

III. 

IV. 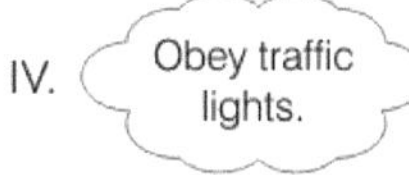

Codes

I II III IV

(a) 

(b) 

(c) 

(d) 

8. Which one of the following safety rules one must follow, while travelling in a school bus?

(a) 

Getting off from a moving bus

(b) 
Placing hands out of the vehicle

(c) 
Disturbing the driver while driving

(d) 

Getting into the bus in a queue

9. In which of the following activities children are following safety rules?

(a) 

(b) 

(c) 

(d) 

10. Match the children with the safety rule they need to follow.

	Column I	Column II
A.		(i) Getting into the bus in a queue
B.		(ii) Cross the road at the zebra crossing
C.		(iii) Walk on the footpath
D.		(iv) Use footbridge to cross the road

Codes

	A	B	C	D
(a)	(iii)	(iv)	(i)	(ii)
(b)	(iii)	(iv)	(ii)	(i)
(c)	(iv)	(iii)	(ii)	(i)
(d)	(iv)	(iii)	(i)	(ii)

11. Why do we empty the room coolers which are not being used?

(a) The water starts smelling bad
(b) Mosquitoes may start growing in the water and cause malaria
(c) The water will become hot
(d) Cockroaches will start living in the water

12. When somebody gets hurt, we need to help that person immediately. This immediate help is called

(a) first aid (b) last aid
(c) safety aid (d) second aid

13. The main aim of giving first aid is to

(a) save lives
(b) keep the person comfortable till medical help arrives
(c) Both (a) and (b)
(d) None of the above

14. We should not touch electric switches with

(a) dry hands (b) bare hands
(c) wet hands (d) left hand

15. What type of clothes should we wear while lighting crackers?

(a) Polyester (b) Nylon
(c) Cotton (d) Terylene

16. We should fly kites

(a) on the terrace (b) in open grounds
(c) in school grounds (d) on the road

17. Which of the following should not be done on a staircase?

Anne fell down the stairs and broke his arm

(a) We should not push or pull other children for fun
(b) We should not lean over the railing of staircase
(c) We should rush down the staircase
(d) We should climb the steps in a line

18. Guess my name.

I am present with you in your school and your mother keep me at home or while travelling. Cotton, scissor, band-aid, antiseptic lotion, etc., are all my friends.

Who am I?

(a) Briefcase
(b) First-aid box
(c) Makeup box
(d) None of these

19. Choose the correct options.

We should not talk on mobile

(a) while watching movie
(b) when in a metro
(c) while driving
(d) when on the footpath

20. Which of the following traffic signal indicate that the pedestrian must not cross the road?

(a) When pedestrian light is green
(b) When pedestrian light is red
(c) When traffic light is red
(d) When traffic light is yellow

21. Which of the following number will you dial to call an ambulance?

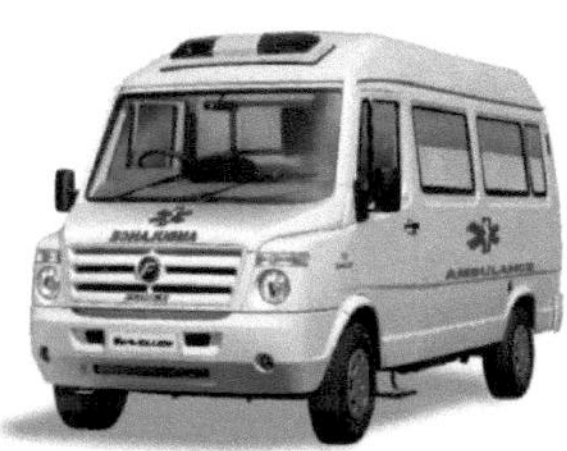

(a) 100 (b) 101
(c) 102 (d) 1098

22. Which of the following activity shows the safety rules?

(a) 

(b) 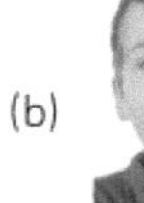 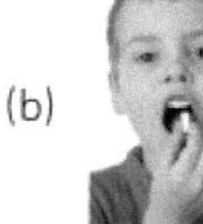

(c) 

(d) 

23. Identify the figure that is not following the safety rules, while playing in the playground.

(a) 

(b) 

(c) 

(d) 

Air and Water

1. Air cannot be seen but we can say that, air is present when we see

(a) 

(b) 

(c) 

(d) All of these

2. Look at the pictures given below.

Sail boat

Windmill

Which common things they all need?

(a) Water
(b) Air
(c) Sun
(d) Wings

3. Look at the figure given below.

Hot air balloon

Which of the following make the hot air balloons to fly?

(a) Water (b) Electricity
(c) Petrol (d) Wind

4. Which of the following is not a source of drinking water?

(a) 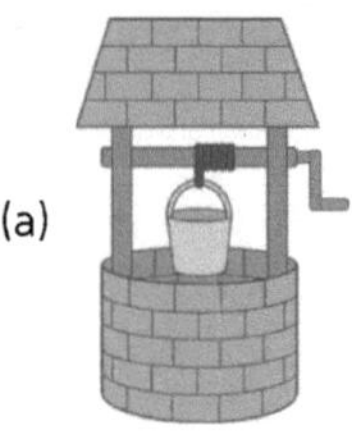
Well

(b) 
Hand pump

(c) 
Seas and oceans

(d) 
Rainwater

5. The movement of water vapours upwards to form clouds and the downward movement of rain forms the

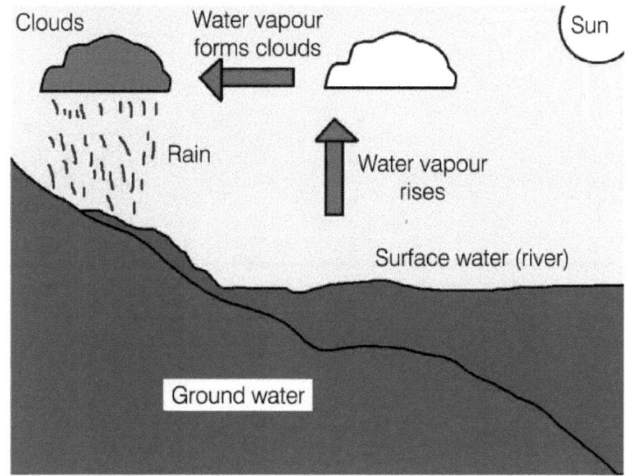

(a) air cycle (b) oxygen cycle
(c) water cycle (d) nitrogen cycle

6. Look at the following pictures and choose the correct options of the given questions.

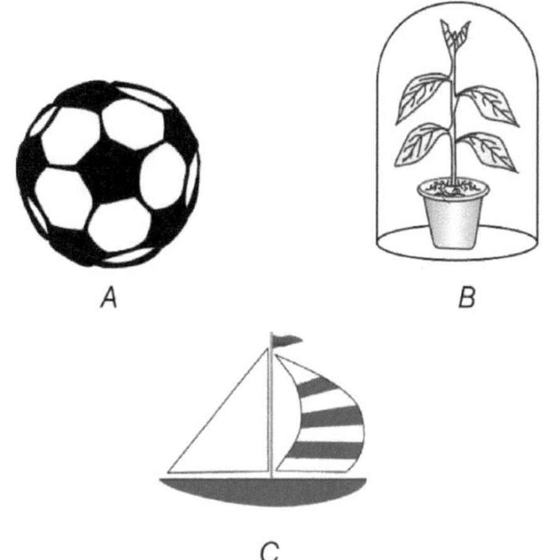

Which picture shows that air occupies space?

(a) Picture *A* (b) Picture *B*
(c) Picture *C* (d) All of these

7. Guess my name.

I flow from mountains as river.

I get collected in seas and oceans.

Who am I?

(a) Air
(b) Soil
(c) Water
(d) Plants

8. Ramu's teacher light a candle and placed it on a table. Simultaneously, she took another candle in a wide container then she light it and cover it with a glass. The flame of the candle covered with glass go out after sometime.

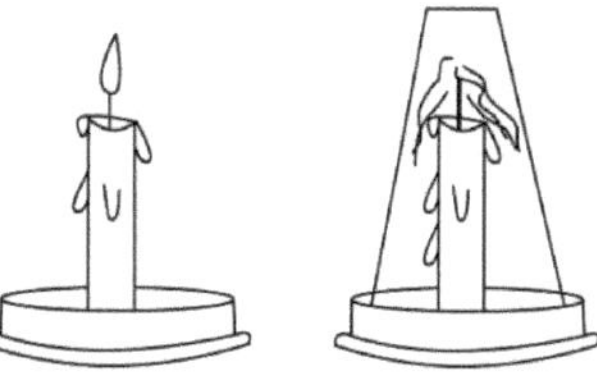

What does this experiment shows?

(a) Candle cannot burn for long time
(b) Air has weight
(c) Air is needed for burning
(d) None of the above

9. Match the following columns.

	Column I		Column II
A.	Breeze	(i)	Healthy
B.	Water vapour	(ii)	Gentle wind
C.	Clean air	(iii)	Present in air
D.	Air fills	(iv)	Space

Codes

	A	B	C	D
(a)	(ii)	(iii)	(i)	(iv)
(b)	(iii)	(i)	(ii)	(iv)
(c)	(iii)	(iv)	(i)	(ii)
(d)	(iv)	(iii)	(i)	(ii)

10. Look at the following pictures and complete the sentence.

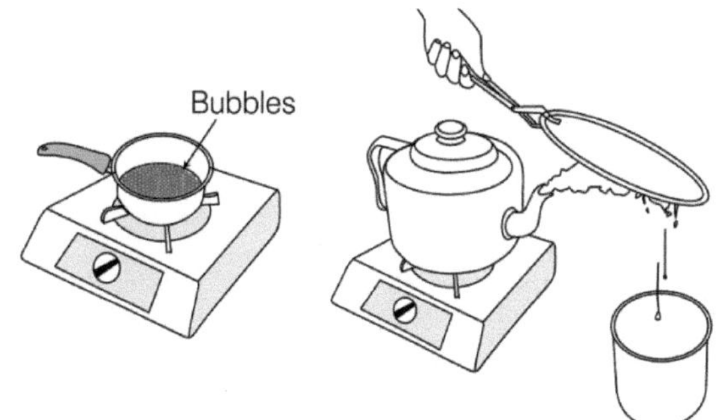

When water is boiled, then it changes into ......*A*...... but when cooled ......*B*...... change into ......*C*...... .

Codes

	A	B	C
(a)	water,	liquid,	solid
(b)	liquid ,	water,	solid
(c)	steam,	steam,	water
(d)	steam,	liquid,	solid

11. Look at the figure carefully and choose the correct option.

We can help to keep the water clean by

(a) not throwing waste into ponds, rivers and lakes
(b) not throwing paints and oils down the sink
(c) planting lots of trees around the water bodies
(d) All of the above

12. Mark 🙂, if true and 🙁, if false.

I. Drinking water should be stored in clean vessels.
II. Containers with drinking water should be covered.
III. It is not our duty to save every drop of water.

(a) I 🙂, II 🙂, III 🙂 (b) I 🙁, II 🙁, III 🙁

(c) I 🙂, II 🙂, III 🙁 (d) I 🙂, II 🙁, III 🙁

13. Three students were talking about the air around us.

Sonal– The air in my school bottle is sweet.

Ritu– Air in my room is blue

Anu–Air in my room is cool.

Whose statement is correct about air?

(a) Sonal (b) Ritu
(c) Anu (d) None of these

14. Dust and smoke makes the air

Dust and smoke

(a) clean (b) polluted
(c) fresh (d) None of these

15. Which of the following things can be done to keep the air clean and fresh?

(a) 

(b) 

(c) 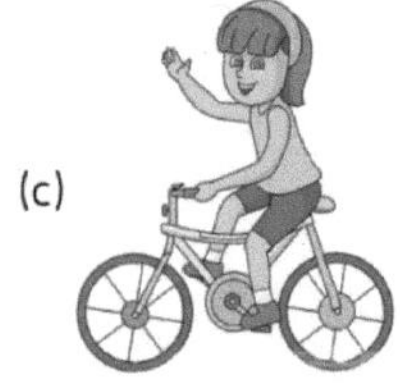

(d) All of these

16. Look at the picture and tell us the three forms of water?

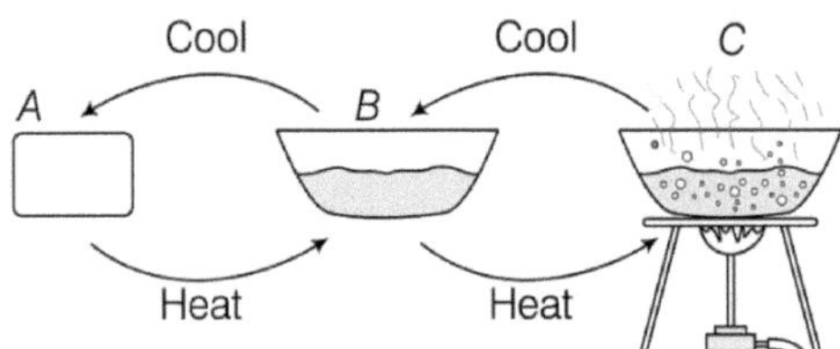

Codes

	A	B	C
(a)	Ice	Water	Water vapour
(b)	Water vapour	Water	Ice
(c)	Water	Ice	Water vapour
(d)	Water vapour	Ice	Water

17. Look at the figure given below.
All these activities shows that air

Air filled in a balloon

Air filled in tyre

Air filled in a football

(a) has weight
(b) occupies space
(c) contains water vapour
(d) moves

18. What energy is used in sail boat, hand gliders and for flying kites to move?

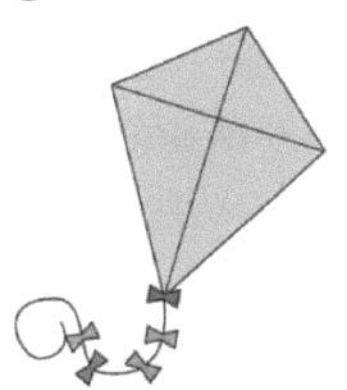
Kite

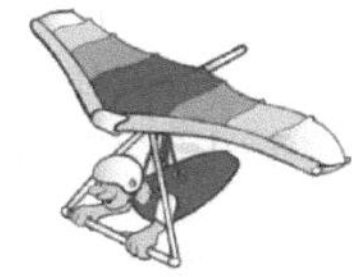
Hand glider

Sail boat

(a) Sun (b) Water
(c) Electricity (d) Wind

19. Match the following columns.

	Column I		Column II
A.	Boiling	(i)	Heats the water in seas
B.	Clouds	(ii)	Water changes into steam
C.	Freezing	(iii)	Water changes into ice
D.	Sun	(iv)	Tiny water drops joined together in air

Codes

	A	B	C	D
(a)	(i)	(iii)	(ii)	(iv)
(b)	(ii)	(iv)	(iii)	(i)
(c)	(ii)	(iii)	(iv)	(i)
(d)	(iii)	(iv)	(ii)	(i)

20. Purification of water can be done by

(a) 
Electronic water filter

(b) 
Boiling water

(c) Both (a) and (b) (d) None of these

21. Which of the following statement is incorrect?
(a) Air is needed for survival of human beings, plants and animals
(b) Moving air is called wind
(c) Air contains dust and smoke only
(d) Air has weight

22. Write one word for the following statement.
We do this to kill germs in water.
(a) Evaporation (b) Cooling
(c) Boiling (d) Storing

23. Look at the following pictures and complete the sentence given below.

In earlier days, trains used to run on
(a) water (b) steam (c) ice (d) electricity

24. Which is the incorrect match?

	Column I	Column II
(a)	Water is present in air in this form	Water vapour
(b)	It fills up ponds, lakes, rivers and seas	Water
(c)	This gives us water in our home	Tap
(d)	We do this to kill germs in water	Freezing

CHAPTER 9

Rocks and Minerals

1. Which of the following is a hard rock?

(a) Granite (b) Coal

(c) Slate (d) Chalk

2. Look at the monument given below. It is made up of

Jama Masjid

(a) granite
(b) marble
(c) sandstone
(d) slate

3. Which of the following rocks is used for producing electricity?

(a) Shale (b) Coal

(c) Marble (d) Limestone

4. Match the following columns.

	Column I		Column II
A.	Taj Mahal	(i)	Gemstone
B.	Red Fort	(ii)	Marble

C.	 Ruby	(iii)	Blackboard
D.	 Slate	(iv)	Sandstone

Codes

	A	B	C	D
(a)	(iv)	(ii)	(i)	(iii)
(b)	(ii)	(iv)	(i)	(iii)
(c)	(iii)	(i)	(iv)	(ii)
(d)	(ii)	(i)	(iii)	(iv)

5. Which of the following pair is incorrect?

(a) Diamond Cutting glass
(b) Mercury Thermometer
(c) Talc Mirror
(d) Quartz Watches

6. Look at the figure given below.

.... is used in lead pencil.

(a) Granite
(b) Chalk
(c) Slate
(d) Graphite

7. Which of these is correct statement about blackboard?

Blackboard

(a) It is made up of slate rock
(b) Slate rock is a type of soft rock
(c) Blackboard is used for writing
(d) All of the above

8. Name the rock or mineral which is used to make floor tiles.

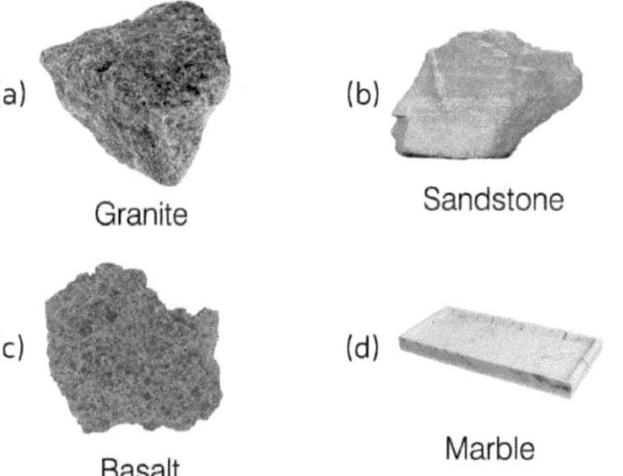

9. Fill in the blanks using correct words.

Ruby and emerald are examples of ......*A*...... which are ......*B*...... and ......*C*...... minerals.

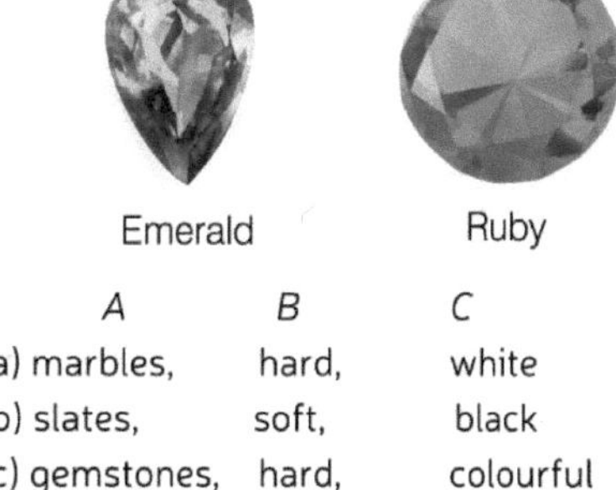

	A	*B*	*C*
(a)	marbles,	hard,	white
(b)	slates,	soft,	black
(c)	gemstones,	hard,	colourful
(d)	marbles,	hard,	colourful

10. Write one word for the following statement.

It is used for cutting glasses.

(a) Granite (b) Slate
(c) Diamond (d) Limestone

11. Guess my name.

I am hard and red colour mineral.

I cut into different shapes and after polishing, I shine.

People use me in making jewellery.

Who am I ?

(a) Emerald (b) Ruby (c) Granite (d) Diamond

12. Which among the following is not a lava rock?

(a) 
Basalt

(b) 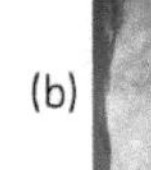 
Marble

(c) 
Obsidian

(d) 
Pumice

13. Soil provides us useful minerals like

(a) diamond and graphite (b) plastic and metals
(c) silk and cotton (d) stones and water

14. Which of the following rocks are used as roofs for buildings?

(a) Granite (b) Sandstone
(c) Slate (d) Marble

15. Mark ☺, if true and ☹, if false.

I. Red Fort is built using sandstone.

II. The Jaipur city is in Rajasthan built by using pink coloured marble.

III. Granite is used in pencils as lead.

Codes

I II III I II III

(a)  (b) 

(c)  (d)  

16. Choose the correct statement.

Slate

(a) I am called the soft rock
(b) I used to make blackboards
(c) My tiles are used as roofs for buildings
(d) All of the above

17. Match the following columns.

	Column I		Column II
A.	Slate	(i)	Lava rock
B.	Limestone	(ii)	Sedimentary rock
C.	Granite	(iii)	Metamorphic rock

Codes

	A	B	C		A	B	C
(a)	(iii)	(ii)	(i)	(b)	(i)	(ii)	(iii)
(c)	(ii)	(iii)	(i)	(d)	(i)	(iii)	(ii)

18. Look at this picture of Earth and tell the *A*, *B* and *C*.

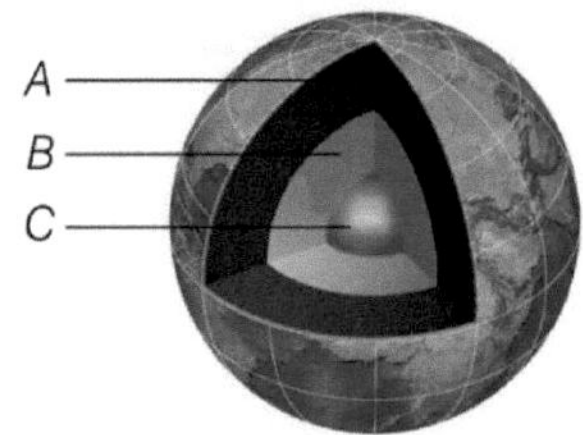

Codes

	A	*B*	*C*
(a)	Core	Mantle	Crust
(b)	Crust	Core	Mantle
(c)	Crust	Mantle	Core
(d)	Mantle	Crust	Core

Our Universe

Direction (Q. Nos. 1-2) *Look at the figure of solar system and answer the following questions by choosing the correct option.*

1. What does planet *A* known as?
(a) Blue planet (b) Black star
(c) Evening star (d) Dull star

2. Name the planet *B* in the solar system.
(a) Neptune (b) Uranus
(c) Saturn (d) Venus

3. Look at the picture and fill in the blanks.

We can see tiny ......*A*...... in the sky. We use a ......*B*...... to see stars.

	A	*B*
(a)	planets,	microscope
(b)	stars,	telescope
(c)	stars,	microscope
(d)	planets,	telescope

4. Earth is also known as 'Blue planet' because of

(a) air (b) water
(c) land (d) gas

5. The largest planet in our solar system is
(a) Jupiter (b) Saturn (c) Neptune (d) Earth

6. Out of Mercury, Venus, Earth and Neptune, which planet is the hottest?
(a) Mercury (b) Venus
(c) Earth (d) Neptune

7. The first man to step on Moon was

(a) Edmund Hillary
(b) Neil Armstrong
(c) Rakesh Pandey
(d) None of the above

8. Which is not a planet ?

(a) Venus
(b) Neptune
(c) Saturn
(d) Moon

9. Which of the following has light of its own?

(a) The Moon
(b) A planet
(c) A star
(d) A satellite

10. Look at the following figures, when length of the shadow changes during the day.

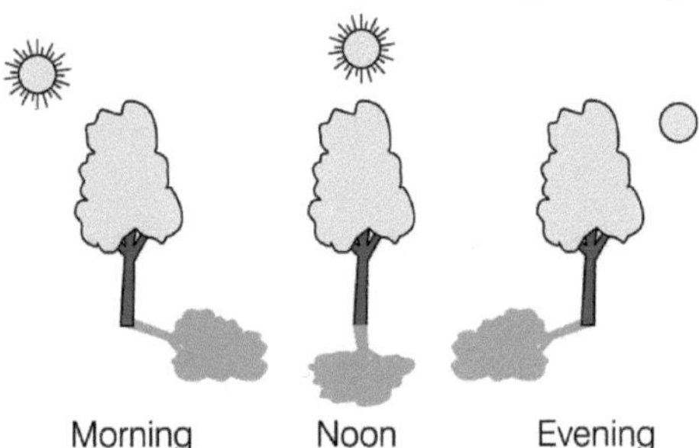

The shadow is formed is every time zone. At what time, the shadow will be longest?

(a) At noon
(b) During morning
(c) During evening
(d) Both during morning and evening

11. The people who study the Sun, Moon, stars and the planets, are known as

(a) scientists
(b) geologists
(c) astronomers
(d) astronauts

12. Which is the brightest planet as viewed from the Earth?

(a) Jupiter
(b) Moon
(c) Venus
(d) Mercury

Direction (Q. Nos. 13-17) *Look at the figure carefully and answer the following questions by choosing the correct option.*

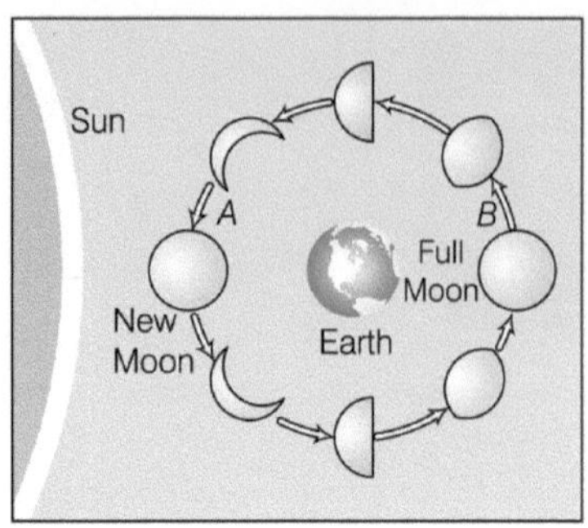

13. The given diagram shows

(a) our solar system
(b) the universe
(c) the phases of the Moon
(d) None of the above

14. The full Moon day (figure *B*) is also known as

(a) Amavasya (b) Purnima
(c) new Moon day (d) crescent Moon

15. The new Moon day (figure *A*) is also known as

(a) full Moon day
(b) crescent Moon
(c) Amavasya
(d) Purnima

16. Who is the head of our solar system?

(a) The Earth (b) Jupiter
(c) The Sun (d) The Moon

17. Guess my name.

A ball without fire.
I turn round and round
You turn with me
And so does the ground
Who am I?

(a) Moon (b) Planet
(c) Earth (d) Mars

18. The following picture shows the eight planets of our solar system.

Choose the correct option.

(a) Planets have a light of their own
(b) They do not reflect the sunlight
(c) They give their light to the Earth
(d) Planets do not have a light of their own

19. Look at the following picture. The person who travels in space is known as

(a) robot
(b) astronaut
(c) scientist
(d) geologist

20. Guess my name.

I am a huge fiery ball.
Far, far away.
When you turn to me,
you have a bright day.
Who am I?

(a) Moon (b) Earth (c) Star (d) Sun

21. Choose the correct statement.

(a) Moon moves round the Earth
(b) Moon does not have light of its own
(c) Moon does not have air or drinking water
(d) All of the above

22. Choose the incorrect match.

(a)	A model of Earth	Globe
(b)	People who visit the space	Astrono outs
(c)	Dwarf planet	Pluto
(d)	Smallest planet	Mercury

23. There are eight planets in our solar system. The correct order of four planets which are nearer to the Sun are

(a) Mercury, Earth, Mars, Jupiter
(b) Mercury, Earth, Mars, Venus
(c) Earth, Mars, Mercury, Venus
(d) Mercury, Venus, Earth, Mars

Practice Set 1

A Test Based on the Whole Content of Class 2nd Science

1. The given food items are

(a) energy giving food (b) body-building food
(c) protective food (d) roadside food

2. Schist is an example of

Schist

(a) metamorphic rock
(b) sedimentary rock
(c) lava rock
(d) None of the above

3. Write the name of the product that we get from the plants that are shown below.

A.  ....

Bamboo plant

B.  ....

Rose plant

C.  ....

Sugarcane plant

	A	*B*	*C*
(a)	Wood	Oil	Sugar
(b)	Wood	Seeds	Sugar
(c)	Paper	Perfumes	Sugar
(d)	Paper	Oil	Cloves

4. Which of the following statements is correct?
(a) It is always safe to play on the road
(b) We must use the footpath while walking
(c) When the traffic signal shows red, the vehicles should move
(d) It is not necessary to obey all the traffic rules

5. Give the one word for the following puzzle.

Who am I?

I help the leaves to rustle and pinwheel to turn.
(a) Gale (b) Storm
(c) Breeze (d) Wind

6. Which of the following yield fibre?

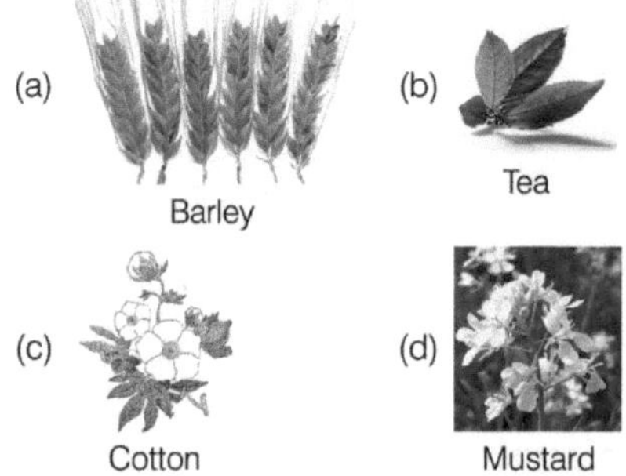

7. The person in the given figure is a/an

(a) doctor
(b) soldier
(c) diver
(d) astronaut

8. Which part of the given plant produces seeds?

(a) *P* (b) *S*
(c) *Q* (d) *R*

9. What causes water to change from one form to another?

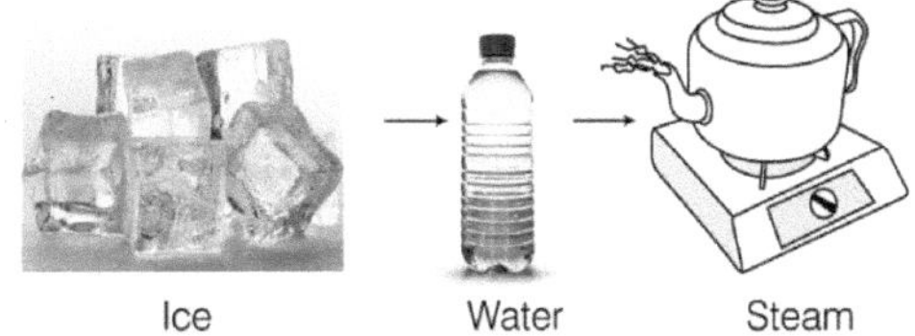

Ice Water Steam

(a) Heating
(b) Cooling
(c) Heating and cooling
(d) None of these

10. Look at the pictures given below. Match the plant with its correct type.

Column I	Column II
A.	(i) Herb
B.	(ii) Shrub
C.	(iii) Tree
D.	(iv) Creeper

Codes

	A	B	C	D		A	B	C	D
(a)	(iv)	(iii)	(ii)	(i)	(b)	(iii)	(iv)	(ii)	(i)
(c)	(iii)	(i)	(iv)	(ii)	(d)	(iv)	(ii)	(i)	(iii)

11. A pond contains clean water. Which of the following activities will produce least pollution of water?
(a) Washing clothes in the pond
(b) Animals bathing in the pond
(c) Washing motor vehicles in the pond
(d) Swimming in the pond

12. Which of the following is incorrectly matched?

(a)  Food stored in a fruit

(b)  Food stored in a stem

(c)  Food stored in seeds (wheat)

(d) 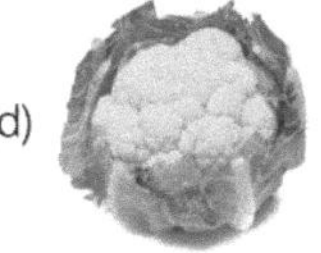 Food stored in flower

13. Which of the following tree gives us gum?
(a) Acacia tree
(b) Coconut tree
(c) Banyan tree
(d) Mango tree

14. Match the following columns.

Column I	Column II
A. Gorilla	(i) Cave
B. Snake	(ii) Den
C. Tiger	(iii) Hole
D. Bear	(iv) Open places

Codes

	A	B	C	D
(a)	(iv)	(iii)	(i)	(ii)
(b)	(ii)	(i)	(iii)	(iv)
(c)	(i)	(iii)	(ii)	(iv)
(d)	(iv)	(iii)	(ii)	(i)

15. Clothes take longer time to dry on a

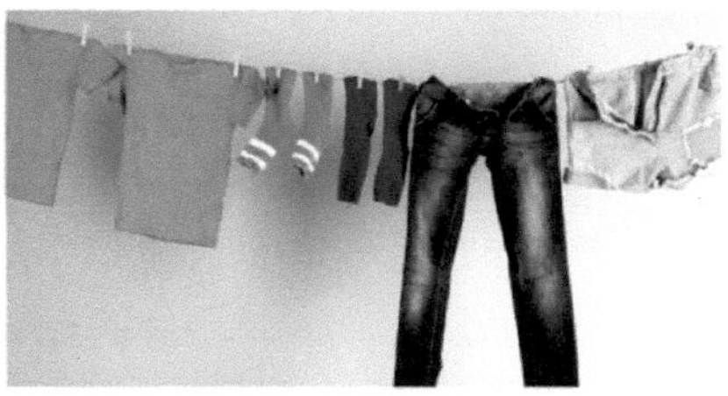

(a) sunny day (b) rainy day
(c) dry day (d) windy day

Practice Set 2

A Test Based on the Whole Content of Class 2nd Science

1. Which of the following is not our sense organ?

(a) 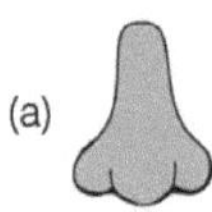

(b) 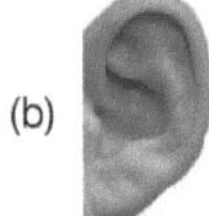

(c) 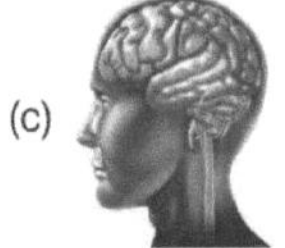

(d) 

2. Which of the following are hard rocks?

(a) 
Sandstone

(b) 
Granite

(c) 
Marble

(d) All of these 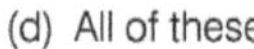

3. Match the animals with the things we get from them and mark the correct option.

Column I		Column I	
A.		(i)	
B.		(ii)	
C.		(iii)	
D.		(iv)	

Codes

	A	B	C	D		A	B	C	D
(a)	(iv)	(iii)	(i)	(ii)	(b)	(iii)	(iv)	(i)	(ii)
(c)	(iii)	(i)	(ii)	(iv)	(d)	(iii)	(i)	(iv)	(ii)

4. Choose the correct option what is posture?
(a) It is a soft part of our body which is below our skin
(b) It is the hard part of our body
(c) It is the position of our body while standing, sitting or walking
(d) It is the framework of bones

5. Fill in the blanks with the correct options.

Sun

Moon

Earth

I. The Sun gives us heat and ....
II. The half of the Earth that faces the Sun has ....
III. We have day and night because the ...... turns.
IV. Moon shines in the light of the ....

Codes

	I	II	III	IV
(a)	energy	day	Moon	Earth
(b)	day	night	Sun	Earth
(c)	light	day	Earth	Sun
(d)	energy	night	Earth	Sun

6. Which of the following animal does not eat the flesh of other animals?

(a) 

(b) 

(c) 

(d) 

7. Which type of clothes would you prefer on a sunny day?
(a) Thick woollen clothes
(b) Raincoat
(c) Light cotton clothes
(d) Silk clothes

8. Sheela's teacher has arranged the apparatus shown below :

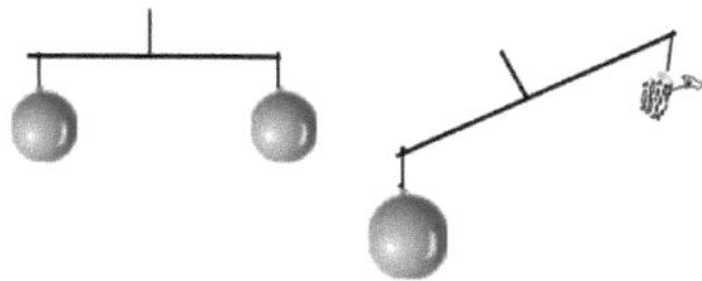

First she below the two balloons and then she prick a pin in one of the balloon what does Sheela's teacher want to convey?

(a) Air cannot be stored
(b) Air is nothing
(c) Air is a simply a gas
(d) Air has weight

9. Which of the following activities is good for reducing air pollution?

(a) 

(b) 

(c) 

(d) Both (a) and (b)

10. Electricity makes many things work in the house. It is also very powerful.

What are methods one should not adopt as it can harm the person?

(a) 
Play with electricity

(b) 
Do not play with fire

(c) 
Wash out for wet floors

(d) None of these

11. Look at the figure given below and choose the correct option.

(a) I am called the white planet
(b) I am the fourth planet
(c) I have air and water
(d) Life is not possible on me

12. For thousands of years people have enjoyed looking at these stars.

In this figure, stars, joined together to get the shape of a large dipper. Name that dipper.

(a) Big bear (b) Big dipper
(c) Ursa minor (d) Orion

13. Which of the following dress represent a Kashmiri dress?

14. Guess my name
Who am I?
These houses are built with sloping roofs, in places where it rains heavily.

(a) Kutcha house (b) Cottage
(c) Stilts (d) Yurt

15. Which of the following activities is a healthy eating habits?

(a) Washing hands before eating
(b) Talking while eating food
(c) Eating stale food
(d) Overeating

Answers and Explanations

1 Living and Non-Living Things

1. (d) Living and non-living things occupy space and have weight.

For example, a dog occupies space and has weight. A table also occupies space and has weight.

Non-living things cannot reproduce and breathe but living things can reproduce and also breathe.

2. (a) There are two kinds of non-living things, natural and man-made.

The Sun, Moon, clouds, rivers and mountains are natural things. Things that are made by man like chairs, tables, computers, televisions etc., are called man-made things.

3. (c) Tongue helps us to taste various things. It also helps us to speak. The food we eat is enjoyed through its taste.

Picture A is a salt, which is salty in taste.

Picture B is a toffee, which is sweet in taste.

Picture C is a lemon, which is sour in taste.

Picture D is a bittergourd, which is bitter in taste.

4. (d) The Sun, Moon and group of stars are non-living things. A herb is a living thing. Plants are small with weak stems and have thin and green stems. They are called herbs.

5. (c) Plants, animals and human beings are living things. Non-living things are of two kinds.

(i) Natural things (ii) Man-made things

6. (d) Living and non-living things occupy space and have weight. These are the two qualities which is common between living and non-living things.

7. (b) These fruits are non-living at this stage. When these are removed from the plants they cannot breathe. So, at this point these fruits are non-living things.

8. (c) Insects like cockroaches and butterflies feel changes around them with the help of their antenna.

9. (d) In the given picture, swings, bicycle, bat, ball, chair, desk, gate are non-living things. But childrens, plants animals and birds are living being.

10. (a) The tyre tube will always be non-living thing. Inflating the tube makes it rounder and bigger by external force. This is not growth.

11. (c) Plants do not have **sense organs** (*B*) but they also **feel** (*A*). Plants grow towards the light. A *Mimosa* plant feels (closes) when touched.

12. (a) A seed is a living thing because it grows into a sapling, which grows into a plant and then into a tree.

13. (d) 'Touch me not' is a plant and shows the features of living beings. It can breathe, grow and shows movement upon touching.

14. (c) Milk is a non-living thing. Tree and men is a living thing. Cooking oil is a non-living thing. Living things are those which can grow, move, can breathe and also have space but non-living things cannot respire and move.

15. (c) Insects breathe through tiny holes in their body. A fish breathes through special structure called gills.

Plants breathe through stomata. Stomata are small openings present mostly on the lower surface of a leaf.

16. (c) Non-living things are clouds, rivers and mountains as they cannot breathe.

17. (c) Skin is involved when Kunal made this prediction. He put his hand is the box and by touching he is able to conclude the nature of the object which is inside the box. Skin helps us in distinguishing whether something is hot, cold, rough or smooth.

18. (d) Non-living things do not need food, air and water. They do not breathe and they do not reproduce. These qualities differs them from living things.

19. (d) All living things produce their own kind. Birds lay eggs.

Cats, dogs and human beings give birth to their young one.

Plants produce seeds, which give rise to a new plant.

20. (a) A butterfly died because there is no **air** in the glass jar. All living things breathe in air. All living beings need air to survive as air is rich in oxygen.

2 Plants

1. The leaves, fruits and seeds of neem tree gives
(c) us medicines. It has antibacterial property.

2. Mint, coriander and tulsi are herbs. Some plants
(d) are small with weak stems. They have thin and green stems. They are called herbs.

3. Plants that grow along the ground are called
(d) creepers.

Plants that climb up taking the support of other plants, sticks or walls are called climbers.

Watermelon is a creeper.

4. Banyan trees have roots growing from their
(c) branches. These trees get modified for their survival. These type of roots help the tree to stand around 100 years.

5. In plants like the ginger, the stem grows
(c) underground and stores extra food.

Carrot and turnip are roots which store food.

In lettuce, leaves store food.

6. A–*Hydrilla* is a water plant. A water plant is a
(a) plant which grow only in the water not on the land.

B–Rose plant is a shrub. These are plants which are not as big as trees. They are lower than a tree and often have smaller stems branching off near the ground. They are called shrubs.

C–Mint is a herb. These plants are small with weak stem. They have thin and green stem.

7. Plant make their own food. The process of
(c) making food by the plants is known as photosynthesis. Germination is the process by which seed grows into seedling.

Breathing is a process by which living things takes oxygen and respire.

8. Cotton fibres comes from the cotton plants,
(a) which are grown in the fields by the farmer.

Jute are obtained from jute fibres.

Wool comes from sheep and leather is obtained from the skin of animals.

9. A–Bamboos are used to make furnitures.
(b) B–Tulsi are used to make medicines.

C–Jasmine are used to make perfumes.

D–Sugarcane are used make sugar.

10. The green leaves use sunlight, water from the
(d) soil, carbon dioxide from air to make food for the plant by the process of photosynthesis.

11. *Cactus* usually grows in desert area. It has
(c) thorns. It can store water in its stem.

These *Cactus* modify its stems into thorns to protect itself from animals.

12. In sugarcane plants, the extra food is stored in
(c) the stem. Stem of the plant get modified to store food.

13. Two climber plants that have weak and soft.
(c) Stems are pea plant and bean plant.

Climbers are the plants which when grows can climb over walls and floors or any other surface for their growth.

14. To make food, a plant uses **sunlight**, water from
(b) the soil, carbon dioxide from air and the process is known as **photosynthesis**.

15. I. Plant grows from **seed**.
(c) II. The fruit grows from the **flower**.

III. Buds grow on the **stem**.

16. A palm is a **tall** tree and palm trees have no
(d) **branches**.

17. Grain is the part we eat in the wheat plant. These
(c) grains are cleaned by the people and then these grains reached the flour mill. From there, we get the flour.

18. Root absorb water and minerals for the growth
(d) of plant. Leaves prepare food for the plant.

19. Roots fix the plant firmly in the soil. They
(a) prevent the plant from falling down. The stem holds the plant upright.

20. *A*–Herbs, very small plants are called herbs.
(c) *B*–Climbers are plant with weak stem.

C–Creeper which grows along the ground.

D–Shrubs are short and bushy plants.

21. I. Plants make the air, clean, fresh and plants
(c) give us shadows. Plants after photosynthesis releases oxygen which is useful for human beings and absorbs carbon dioxide (harmful for living being). Thus, making the air clean and fresh.

22. (b) Money plant and grapevine are examples of climbers because they climb up taking the support of other plants, sticks or walls.

Creepers plant grow along the group. Herbs are very small plant and shrubs are short and bushy plant.

23. (b) **Correct statement** In cabbage, leaves store the food. That's why we eat the leaves of such plants. Cabbage is not a flower.

3 Animals

1. (d) Milk giving animals produces milk. The animals are cow, buffaloes, camel and goat.

2. (c) Dog is a pet animal. Rat, polar bear and squirrel are non-pet animals.

Pet animals are those animals which lives with human being in the home. They are very caring and loving.

3. (b) (i) A puppy is a baby of dog.

(ii) A colt is a baby of horse.

(iii) A kid is a baby of goat.

(iv) A calf is a baby of cow.

4. (b) All animals need protection and care. Domestic animals serve us well, if we take good care of them.

5. (c) Rat, wolf, pig and bear are omnivores. Omnivore animals are those animals, who eat both plants as well as meat.

Carnivore animals are those animals, who eat only meat. Herbivore animals are those animals who eat only plants.

6. (d) Animals like elephant, cow and rhinoceros are herbivores but cheetah is carnivores.

7. (a) A–Rabbit love to eat carrot.

B–Cat love to drink milk.

C–Goat love to eat grass.

D–Elephant love to eat bushes.

8. (d) The animals which need for transportation and for field work are known as **draught** animals. These animals are very useful for human welfare.

9. (c) Kangaroos are found only in Australia and they carry their young ones called joey in a pouch.

10. (a) A–Dog lives in a kennel.

B–Horse lives in a stable.

C–Lions lives in a den.

D–Cow lives in a shed.

11. (d) Sheep, goat and yak are wool yielding animals.

12. (d) Bees make honey from the nectar of flowers.

13. (b) A tiger's young one is called a cub. Goat's young one is called a kid, lamb is a young one of sheep and a zebra's young one is called a colt.

14. (c) In the picture *A*, sheep are there. These sheeps provide us wool. In picture *B*, silkworm and cocoons are there. They provide us silk threads.

15. (d) Bullock, camels, donkeys, mules, ponies and elephant are used to carry loads. Dogs are used to guard houses and farms.

16. (b) In the picture, vulture is the bird. The food it like to eat are small animals and meat.

17. (b) A–Owl makes a sound as hoot-hoot.

B–Koel makes a sound as coohoo-coohoo.

C–Crow makes a sound as caw-caw.

D–Sparrow makes a sound as chirp-chirp.

18. (b) Dog eat vegetables and bones. He lives in a kennel. He guard our home. He says bow-bow.

19. (c) A cockroach have six legs. It have two antennae also. It is an insect and also a pest at our home.

20. (a) Animals who eat only plants or leaves are called herbivores animals.

Rabbit, rhinoceros, elephant, deer, cow and goat are herbivores.

21. (c) Tortoises are protected from predators (enemies) by a thick shell on its body.

22. (c) Snake, cheetah, pangolin and rhinoceros are animals which live on land. But fish and dolphin live in water only.

23. Leather things are made from the skin of
(c) animals.

24. I. Dairy animals does not give meat. They give
(d) us milk.

II. Carrot is the favourite food of rabbit.

III. Eggs lays by hen are rich in proteins.

25. Birds like humming bird and Sun birds have
(a) long and pointed beaks. Their beaks help them to suck nectar from flowers.

26. (i) A group of elephants are called **parade**.
(c) (ii) A group of emus are called **mob**.

(iii) A group of fish are called **school**.

(iv) A group of bacteria are called **colony**.

27. A–In humans, the exchange of gases between
(c) the systems happens in the lungs.

B–Fishes lives in the water and respire through gills.

C–*Amoeba* breathe through body surfaces.

D–Insect breathe through spiracles.

28. There are four animal words in the box.
(b) They are as follows :

M	L	T	U	J	K	O	**C**	**O**	**W**
B	F	**B**	**U**	**F**	**F**	**A**	**L**	**O**	X
U	N	I	M	F	O	N	D	W	E
F	I	H	**G**	**O**	**A**	**T**	R	S	T
I	A	R	P	G	N	C	**O**	**X**	K
T	S	Q	B	T	L	U	M	J	Y

(i) Cow (ii) Buffalo

(iii) Ox (iv) Goat

4 Human Body

1. Skin and eyes both the sense organs helps the
(d) body. When Ramu got injured immediately he had removed the hand and eyes were able to recognize the redness due to the burn.

2. Lungs are used in the breathing process. Large
(b) intestine is used in the excretion process.

Kidneys are used in the urinary system. Heart are used in the circulatory system for the circulation of blood.

3. Brain is the organ that control all our actions
(c) like seeing, hearing, walking and learning. Brain is the controller of whole body.

4. Our skin help us to feel temperature, hot or cold
(d) in the body.

Tongue helps us to taste, eyes helps us to see and ears helps us to hear.

5. A–Nose help us to smell. It can smell the
(a) fragrance of 'agarbatti'.

B–Ears help us to hear. By using these, we can listen the songs.

C–Eyes help us to see. By using these, we can read the books.

D–Tongue help us to taste. By using these, we can taste the cake.

6. The given organ is brain and it is protected in
(a) skull. The brain can be compared to a computer. It controls all of the body system.

7. (a) Our nose help us to smell.
(c) (b) Our skin help us to feel temperature, touch, pain .

(c) Our tongue helps us to taste .

(d) Our eyes help us to see.

8. We have two eyes, two ears, two legs and two
(d) hands in our body.

9. The given system represents the digestive
(c) system. It consists of mouth, foodpipe, liver, stomach and large intestine. This system helps the body to digest the food and get energy.

10. The part *A* is a skull while part *B* are ribs. Skull
(c) protects the brain and is the hardest part. Ribs protect the internal organs of the body.

11. There are 206 bones in our body. When all
(c) bones are arranged in a proper way, they form a skeletal system.

12. The main function of respiratory system is to
(c) take **oxygen** and give out **carbon dioxide** and the process is known as **breathing.**

13. (c) The main function of heart is to pump blood in the whole body.

Heart is the major organ which takes impure blood from body and then, purifies it. After that, it has been circulated over the body.

14. (c) I. Food helps us to grow.

II. We see with our eyes.

III. We feel things with our skin.

15. (b) For breathing process, the organ involved is lung not ribs. Ribs gives shape to the body and also protect internal organs of the body.

Heart helps in the pumping of blood stomach helps in the digestion of food. Brain helps in the thinking process.

16. (d) The **joint** is a place where two bones meet.

It helps in the movement of bones.

17. (c) Our heart has cardiac muscles and they do not need any rest and they work non-stop throughout our life. It is the main organ of the body.

18. (b) All the muscles in our body form muscular system. Muscles cover the skeleton and are attached to bones.

19. (d) Skeletal system gives shape and support to our body. It protects the internal organs of the body (such as heart, liver and lungs).

20. (c) The correct statement is

Skeletal system gives shape and support to our body. All other statements are correct.

21. (c) The given diagram shows the stomach. Stomach is the main part which is involved in the digestion process. It helps to digest the food. Stomach releases acid which breaks down the food into simpler pieces.

22. (c) Respiratory system helps in breathing. It has nose, lungs. The respiratory system comprises the lungs and the passages that lead to and from them. This system is responsible for exchange of gases that we call breathing.

23. (b) The correct statements is

Muscles cover the skeleton and are attached to bones.

There are about 640 muscles in our body.

Skeletal system gives shape and support to our body.

24. (c) The two organs located in our chest are heart and lungs. The ribcage protect the heart and the lungs. (Stomach and intestine are present below the chest.)

25. (d) Head is the body part, which has all the sense organs present in it. There are five sense organs which help us to see, smell, touch, taste and hear. They are skin, nose, mouth, ears and eyes.

5 Food and Nutrition

1. (d) We need food to live and grow. Food provides us energy to work and play and to remain healthy.

2. (c) Most of the food, which we eat comes from plants and animals. Plants are the major source of food for human beings and other animals. Animals provide us food materials such as milk, eggs, chicken, meat, fish, etc.

3. (c) We get carbohydrates from rice, potato, wheat and fats from butter, ghee, etc. Carbohydrates and fats give us energy.

4. (c) Fruits, vegetables and green leaves provide us vitamins and minerals. These protect us from illness. That's why they are called as protective food. They keep our eyes, skin and gums healthy.

5. (a) Plants gives us fruits and vegetables. Several spices, pulses and herbs are also obtained from plants. Animals gives us meat, egg, milk, etc.

6. (a) Boiled water is better than normal water because boiling kills microbes. Boiled water is good for health. It reduces the chances of infection.

7. (a) **Sense organs** are known as gateway of knowledge. By using all the sense organs, we are able to engulf the knowledge.

Eyes helps to see.

Ears helps to hear.

Tongue helps to speak.

8. (d) The body building foods (proteins) like milk, eggs, chicken, fish, etc., help us to build our muscles and body to grow.

Bread and rice are energy giving food and fruits are called protective food.

9. Pizza, hot dogs, french fries, popcorn, etc., are
(b) examples of junk food. These are to be taken occasionally. Otherwise, it causes obesity.

10. Pizza, burger and chocolates are junk food. Fruit
(d) such as apple, (is a) healthy food.

11. Correct statements are
(c)
I. Wash fruits and vegetables before eating.
II. Cereals are plants products. They are obtained from plants.
III. All vegetables should not be taken as raw, it should be cooked before eating.

12. The sprouts contain more vitamins, which
(c) makes them a more nutritious food. Sprouts taken in breakfast makes us more energetic.

13. Apple, papaya and pomegranate are protective
(d) in nature. They are called as protective food. All fruits are rich in vitamins, minerals, carbohydrates, etc. Hence, they are protective.

14. Nuts are fruits with hard cover or shell.
(d) Sometimes dried seeds are also called nuts. They are very healthy when eaten raw and gives a lot of energy.

15. People who eat fish, meat and chicken are called
(b) non-vegetarian.
People who do not eat fish, meat and chicken are called vegetarian. They only eat vegetables and fruits.

16. Eggs are not fatty food. They are body building
(d) food. They help in the growth of the body. They also help in the repairing of injured parts.

17. Minerals does not give energy. They are got
(b) from both plants and animals. They are not destroyed during food preparation. They help in maintaining water balance in the body.

18. A–Milk is rich in calcium.
(b) B–Dal and roti is rich in carbohydrate.
C–Eggs are rich in protein.
D–Cold drinks are junk food.

19. Good habits are:
(d)
(a) Wash your hands after you use the toilet.
(b) Kep your nails trimmed and clean.
(c) Brush your teeth twice a day.

20. Teeths helps in the chewing of food and cause
(a) the first digestion of food.
When food reached the mouth, it breaks down to smaller units with the help of teeth.

21. Mummy says us to eat green vegetables like
(a) spinach because they are protective foods. Green leafy vegetables protect us bacteria, viruses and other infections.

22. Milk is called a complete food because it helps
(d) us to grow, it protects us from falling sick and it gives us energy to work and play.
It is a body building food. It is also a protective food and it is also energy giving food.

23. Tomato soup is made from tomatoes. Bread is
(d) made from flour. Thus, tomato soup, bread and chick peas are obtained from plants.
Omelette, chicken and milk are obtained from animals.

24. Milk is called a complete food. It is rich in
(d) proteins, vitamins and useful minerals. A vegetarian diet includes only fruits, vegetables, pulses and milk.
Vitamins and minerals protect us from diseases.

25. A–Energy giving food are rice and bread.
(a) B–Roadside food are covered with dust and flies.
C–We should take three meals in a day.
D–Healthy foods are fruits and vegetables.
E–Oily food are spicy fried potatoes.

26. We should drink plenty of water to stay healthy.
(c) Never throw the waste/stale food around. Always use a dustbin.

27. Fruits and vegetables are protective food. Sugar
(b) or sweets are energy giving food, chicken and meat are body building food.

28. If raw food items are cooked, then there
(b) protective nutrients may be lost due to heat.
Eating raw food is also tastier and full of nutrients.

29. A–Children should not play with sharp objects.
(c) This can cause accidents.
Good habits are:
B–Trim your nails.
C–Brush your teeth.
D– Take bath regularly.

30. The diagram shows the food pyramid. In this
(b) diagram, different types of foods are categorised as fats and sugar, dairy products, fruits and vegetables, grains, cereal and pulses.

6 Housing and Clothing

1. (b) A hut, tent house and a yurt are temporary house and these houses are not strong. A house made up of bricks, cement and steel is a strong house.

2. (b) Soldiers and construction workers live in a tent house. A tent house is made of canvas. It can be folded and carried along easily.

3. (c) Eskimos who live in very cold, snow bound regions make igloos from snow to live in. These igloos are warm from inside and protect the eskimos from cold. While kutcha house is made up of mud and clay. Pucca house is made up of cement, bricks and iron.

4. (c) Raincoat and gumboots protect us from rain. We also use an umbrella when we go out in the rain.

5. (d) The picture is a building. They have many homes each of them is called a flat. These houses are very strong and are made from bricks, cement and steel.

6. (a) A–Squirrel built its house on the bark of a tree.

B–Flying birds usually made nests.

C–Snake makes houses in the hole.

D–Lion lives in den.

E–Butterfly lives on the flower.

7. (d) The given picture is a house which is known as stilt. These houses are raised from the ground level on bamboo stilts. These houses are made in areas, where it rains heavily. This does not let the water or snakes enter the house.

8. (c) The incorrect statement is (c), because kutcha house is made up of mud, grass, bamboo, etc.

9. (c) A tent house is made of canvas. It can be folded and carried along easily. Campers, nomads, soldiers and construction workers use this type of house.

10. (a) A yurt is not a permanent house. It is made up of bamboo. It is a type of traditional tent used in some regions.

11. (c) We wear thin cotton clothes on hot days as they keep our body cool.

12. (b) We share our houses with some unwanted visitors. These animals are not our pets. They are called pests. Example cockroaches, lizards, mosquitoes, rats.

13. (b) The correct statements are

I. Kutcha houses are not strong only pucca houses are strong.

II. A hut is made up of materials like grass, mud, bamboo, straw, etc.

14. (d) The picture shows the winter season. In this season, we wear sweaters, gloves, etc., to keep ourselves warm. Cold, dry air blows in this season. In this season, light fire helps us to keep us warm.

15. (b) A–Cotton is the fabric that keeps us cool in summer.

B–Wool is the hair of animals which is used to make the clothes.

C–Waterproof material which does not let water to pass through.

16. (b) A–Shirts are made from cotton. The cotton is taken from cotton plants.

B–Jute bags are made from jutes. These jutes are taken from jute plants.

C–Sweaters are made up from wool. The wool is obtained from sheep.

D–Silk sarees are made from silk threads. The silk threads are obtained from silkworms.

17. (c) (a) People living in houseboats move in and out of their houses in shikaras.

(b) Caravan is a house on wheels that can be attached to a truck and moved from one place to another.

(c) Tents can be folded and packed.

(d) Igloo houses are made from blocks of ice.

18. (b) Kutcha house is made of mud, straw, stones, bamboo, etc.

19. (c) Fibres that are made by man are called man-made fibres. Nylon, polyester, rayon and acrylic are examples of man-made fibre.

20. (d) In pictures, there are three animals mountain goat, sheep and mountain camel. These animals helps to get wool fibres. The wool is obtained from the skin of these animals. These are used to make woollen clothes.

21. (a) A,B–Sweater and gloves are used in winters.
C–Short pants are used in summers.
D–Raincoats are used in rainy seasons.

22. (a) Cement is used to make the walls of constructions. Wood, rubber and plastic are not used to make the walls of constructions, because wood is supported material.

7 Safety and First Aid

1. (d) Avoid touching pointed or sharp edged objects like needles, knifes, blades, etc. These objects may bruise you and lead to injury.

2. (a) The black and white strips on the roads are called zebra crossing. Always cross the road at the zebra crossing.

3. (a) In figure (a) a traffic inspector is instructing the public about the traffic.
In figure (b) a police inspector is there.
In figure (c) a soldier is there.

4. (d) While riding a bicycle on the road, one should always keep to the left of the roadside to stay safe and alert.

5. (d) When we go to swimming, then we should swim only in the presence of an adult. We should use floaters or swimming tubes, while learning swimming. Never go to the deep inside of a pool.

6. (c) The skull and crossbones, a common symbol is today generally used as a warning of danger, particularly in regard to poisonous and dangerous things.

7. (b)
I. We should not swing on windows. This can cause accidents.
II. We should not play on road. For playing, parks are made.
III. Hold hands of parents on roads.
IV. Obey traffic lights.

8. (d) The following safety rule one must follow while travelling in a bus.
- Stand in a queue, while waiting for or boarding the bus.
- Stay seated while the bus is moving.
- Talk softly to the bus driver, so that he can concentrate on driving.
- Do not lean out of a moving bus.

9. (c) Figure (a) Do not rush through a gate to enter or get out of your school. You may hit the gate and get hurt.
Figure (b) Do not climb on the furniture in the classroom.
Figure (d) Do not rundown the staircase.
Figure (c) You should always walk on the pavement or on the safe side of the road.

10. (c) In figure A, people are using footbridges to cross the road. This is a safety measure for crossing the road.
In figure B, boy is walking on the footpath. One should always use footpath while walking on road.
In figure C, people are crossing the road at the zebra crossing.
In figure D, children are getting into the bus in a queue.

11. (b) We should empty room coolers when they are not in use because the water in coolers can breed the mosquitoes and cause malaria.

12. (a) The immediate help given to an injured person is called first aid.

13. (c) The main aim of giving first aid is to save lives and keeps the person comfortable till medical help arrives.
First aid is the first help which is given to the injured person.

14. (c) Do not touch electric wires, switches, electric gadget and plugs with wet hands. You might get an electric shock.

15. (c) While lighting crackers, we should use cotton clothes as this does not catch fire polyester, nylon and terylene are synthetic clothes. They can easily catch fire.

16. (b) We should always fly kites in open ground not on the terrace or on the road. Flying kites on the terrace is dangerous as chances of slipping or falling down may occur.

17. (c) The correct statement is (c) because we should not rush down the staircase otherwise we may fall and can get injury.

18. (b) A box that contains things like cotton, antiseptic lotion and band-aid needed to give first-aid to an injured person is called a first-aid box.

19. (c) We should not speak on the mobile while driving.

20. (b) When the traffic signal is red, it indicates that the pedestrian must not cross the road. It says 'Stop'.

When pedestrian light is green, it says that people can cross the road. When pedestrian light is yellow, people should wait.

21. (c) Emergency numbers are

100– Local police

101– Fire service

1098– Child helpline number

22. (c) The correct safety rules are :

(a) In the playground keep away from thorny plants.

(b) You should not take medicines without your elders permission.

(d) Never jump on the desks inside the classroom.

23. (b) The following are the safety rules one should follow in the playground while playing.

- Do not push each other while playing or on swings.
- Learn and follow the rules of whichever game you play.
- Wait for your turn at the swing, at the *sew-saw*, infact everywhere.

8 Air and Water

1. (d) Air cannot be seen but we do see the pages of our notebooks fluttering or the curtains blowing. We also feel the heat waves on a hot and windy summer afternoon.

2. (b) Moving air is called wind. Wind can help us in many ways.

Wind moves a sail boat.

Wind turns the blades of a windmill.

3. (d) Wind makes the hot air balloons to fly. With the help of wind, the air balloons are able to fly. These air balloons exert pressure against it and then easily fly.

4. (c) Rain fills up the rivers, lakes, ponds and wells. This water is then used by human beings and animals.

Sea water is not fit for drinking, as it is salty.

5. (c) The movement of water vapours upwards to form clouds and the downward movement of rain forms the **water cycle.** Water from sea and rivers gets evaporated into water vapour called as evaporation. When these water vapour get condensed into water, then it is called as condensations.

6. (a) Things like tyres, balloon, football, etc., grow in size when air is filled in them. This shows that air occupies space.

7. (c) Water flow from mountains as river. It get collected in seas and oceans.

8. (c) The experiment shows that air is needed for burning. This is because the candle had used up all the oxygen in the glass and when all oxygen is used up, it is not able to burn anymore and get extinguished.

9. (a) A–A **gentle wind** is called **breeze**.

B–**Air** contains water in the form of **water vapour**

C–We should breathe **clean air** to stay **healthy**.

D–**Air fills** the **space**.

10. (c) When we heat water in a vessel, we see bubbles forming in the water. These bubbles then rise and come out as steam or water vapour. When this steam comes in contact with a cold plate, it cools down and turns back into drops of water.

11. (d) The picture shows the improper dumping of garbage.

We can help to keep the water clean by not throwing waste into ponds, rivers and lakes. Also, do not throw paints and oils down the sink. We should plant lot of trees around the water bodies.

12. (c) I. Drinking water should be stored in clean vessels.

II. Containers with drinking water should be covered.

III. It is only our duty to save every drop of water.

13. (c) Anu's statement is correct about air. Sonal's statement is wrong as air has no taste. Air is present all around. It does not have colour, taste and feeling. We cannot feel the air. Air is required by all the living organisms.

14. (b) Dust and smoke makes the air polluted. The dust, smoke and germs originate from the factories and vehicles. These things causes air pollution.

15. (d) We should breathe in clean air to stay healthy. Things that can be done to keep the air clean are

- Do not burn wood.
- Plant a tree.
- Walk or use a bicycle instead of other vehicles.

16. (a) When **ice** get heated, it melts and **water** is formed. This water when get heated, it turns into **water vapour**.

Similarly, when water vapour gets cooled, it gives water and when this water get cooled it forms ice.

17. (b) Air takes up space. When we blow air into a balloon, it fills the space inside the balloon. Air filled in a football and tyres takes up the space inside and gives them their shape.

18. (d) Air or wind energy is used in sail boat, hand gliders and for flying kites.

19. (b) A–During boiling, water changes into steam.

B–When tiny drops joined together in air, they form clouds.

C–During freezing, water changes into ice.

D–Sun heats the water in seas.

20. (c) The water in the taps is not safe for drinking. We should use good quality water filters or boil this water before drinking. These filters or boiling kills the germs which is present in them.

21. (c) The incorrect statement is

Air contains dust and smoke only.

Corrected statement is

Air is a mixture of gases such as water vapour, smoke, dust and germs.

22. (c) Ground water is not safe for drinking. This water contains germs, which can make us fall sick. To kill the germs, we should always boil water before drinking.

23. (b) In earlier days, trains used to run on steam. Steam is a form of air. Steam energy is used to move the engine.

24. (d) Freezing is not the correct method to kill the germs in water. Boiling is method which is used to kill the germs. We should always boil water before drinking.

Other matches are correct.

9 Rocks and Minerals

1. (a) Some rocks are very hard to break. They are called hard rocks. Granite, marble and sand stones are hard rocks. Coal, slate and chalk are soft rocks and break easily.

2. (c) The Jama Masjid and Red Fort in New Delhi are built using sandstones. Sandstone is a soft stone that is made when sand grains cement together.

3. (b) Coal is used to producing electricity. It is a valuable non-renewable mineral resource. It is a sedimentary rock. It is made of organic carbon which is the actual remains of dead plants.

4. (b) A–Taj Mahal is made up of marble.

B–Red Fort is made up of sandstone.

C–Ruby is a gemstone.

D–Blackboard is made up of slate.

5. (c) The incorrect pair is talc and mirror. As talc is made up of talc powder. It is made up of silicates.

6. (d) Graphite is used in lead pencil. When coal is subjected to more heat and pressure, it can become graphite. So, graphite is a form of carbon.

7. Blackboard is made up from slate rock. It is a
(d) type of soft rock. It is used for writing.

8. Granite is a very hard rock. It can be polished
(a) smooth and is mainly used for making floor tiles, kitchen slabs and walls of buildings.

9. Ruby and emerald are examples of **gemstone**
(c) which are **hard** and **colourful** minerals.

Crystals are those minerals that have had the chance to grow in shape over millions of years.

10. Diamond is used for cutting glasses. It is the
(c) hardest known mineral. Diamond is also the form of carbon. When coal is subjected to more heat and pressure, it can become diamond.

11. Ruby is the hard and red colour mineral. It can
(b) cut into different shapes and after polishing, it usually shines. People use it in making jewellery.

12. Marble is not a lava rock. It is an example of a
(b) metamorphic rock formed from the sedimentary rock, limestone.

Lava rock is formed when lava cools down on the surface. Basalt, obsidian and pumice are lava rocks.

13. Soil provides us useful minerals like diamond and
(a) graphite. These rocks and minerals are formed due to more heat and pressure.

14. Slate tiles are used as roofs for buildings.
(c) Granite is used for making floor tiles.

Sandstone are used for buildings and statues.

Marble is used for making buildings, floors of houses, etc.

15. I. Red Fort is built using sandstone.
(c) II. The Jaipur city is in Rajasthan built by using pink coloured marble.

III. Graphite is used in pencils as lead.

Granite is used for making floor tiles.

16. Slate is called the soft rock. It is used to make
(d) blackboards. Its tiles are used as roofs for buildings.

17. A–Slate is a metamorphic rock.
(a) B–Limestone is a sedimentary rock.

C–Granite is a lava rock.

18. A–**Crust** is a outermost covering of the Earth.
(c) B–**Mantle** lies below the crust.

C– **Core** is mainly made of iron and nickel.

It lies deep inside the crust.

10 Our Universe

1. Planet *A* is a Venus. It is also known as evening
(c) star. It is the brightest planet when seen from the surface of the Earth.

2. The planet *B* in the solar system is Saturn.
(c) This planet has rings and due to the presence of rings it is unique.

3. We see tiny **stars** in the sky. We use a
(b) **telescope** to see stars. Telescope is a device which is use to see distant objects.

4. Earth is also known as 'Blue planet' because of
(b) presence of **water**. About three-fourth of its surface is water and one-fourth is land.

5. Jupiter is the largest planet in our solar system
(a) and Saturn is the second largest planet.

6. Mercury is the nearest planet to the Sun but is
(b) not as hot as Venus. The surface temperature of Venus is higher than that of Mercury.

7. The first man who stepped on the surface of the
(b) Moon was Neil Armstrong.

8. Mercury, Venus, Earth, Mars, Jupiter, Saturn,
(d) Uranus and Neptune are eight planets of our solar system.

The Moon is a natural satellite of the Earth.

9. A star is a big ball of burning gases which gives
(c) out both heat and light.

10. We can see that the shadows are longest during
(d) the morning and evening and shortest during the afternoon.

11. Astronomers are people who study the Sun,
(c) Moon, stars and the planets.

12. Venus, also known as evening star, is brightest
(c) planet as seen from the surface of the Earth. It has an apparent brightness magnitude of 4.4.

13. (c) The different shapes of the Moon, as seen on different days are known as phases of the Moon.

14. (b) The full Moon day which is figure *B* is also known as Purnima. When the is on the opposite side of the Earth, we can see the full lighted surface. This is the full Moon or Purnima.

15. (c) Full Moon day is called Purnima. New Moon day is called Amavasya. Purnima and Amavasya come once every month.

16. (c) The Sun is our nearest star. It is a huge ball of burning gases that gives us light and heat. It is the head of the solar system.

17. (c) Earth is a ball without fire. It turn round and round. We turn with it and also with the ground. When Earth moves, then we also moves with it.

18. (d) Planets do not have a light of their own. They reflect the sunlight that falls on them. This make planets glow.

19. (b) The astronaut is the person who reaches on the Moon, wears special space suit that protect him from the harmful rays of the Sun.

20. (d) Sun is a huge fiery ball. It gives a bright day.

21. (d) Moon moves round the Earth. It does not have light of its own. It does not have air or drinking water.

22. (b) People, who visit the space are called astronauts. The astronauts are those who go to the Moon wear special space suits that protect them from the harmful rays of the Sun.

23. (d) Eight planets in the solar system are Mercury, Venus, Earth, Mars, Jupiter, Saturn, Uranus and Neptune.

Practice Set 1

1. (b) Food items like milk, fish, meat, eggs, pulses, green peas, chicken help us to grow. They make our bones and muscles strong. These food items are called body-building food. Protective food protect us from infection. Energy giving food gives us energy for the good functioning of body.

2. (a) Schist is an example of metamorphic rock. Metamorphic rocks are originally igneous or sedimentary. When the Earth's crust moves, it causes rocks to get squeezed so hard that the heat causes the rock to change.

3. (c) A–Wood of some plants such as bamboo and pine is used to make paper.

B–Flowers of rose plant are used to make soaps, shampoos and perfumes.

C–We get jaggery and sugar from sugarcane.

4. (b) The correct statements are

It is not safe to play or run on the road.

When the traffic signal shows red, the vehicles should stop.

It is necessary to obey all the traffic rules because road accidents happen when people do not follow the traffic rules.

5. (c) A gentle wind is called breeze. Leaves of a tree rustle when a breeze blows.

A strong wind is called a gale.

A very strong and noisy wind is called a storm.

6. (c) Cotton plant yields fibre.

Barley yields maize.

Tea plants yields tea leaves.

Mustard plants yields mustard oil.

7. (c) The person in the given figure is a diver. Diver dives inside the water. He explores the world of the sea.

8. (a) Seeds are mostly contained in the fruits. Different fruits contain different types and number of seeds.

9. (c) Water changes from one form to another when it is heated or cooled. Ice, water and water vapour or steam are the three different forms of water.

10. (c) Picture-A is of a tree.

Picture-B is of a herb.

Picture-C is of a creeper.

Picture-D is of a shrub.

11. (*d*) Swimming in the pond will not pollute water. Washing clothes in the pond, animal both and washing motor vehicles will produce pollution.

12. (*b*) Carrot is a modified root, not a modified stem. Modified root stored food in them.

13. (*a*) We get a sticky juice from a tree named acacia, which is used to make gum.

14. (*d*) A–Gorilla lives in open places.

B–Snake lives in a hole.

C–Tiger lives in a den.

D–Bear lives in a cave.

15. (*b*) Clothes dry quickly on sunny day and windy day. Rainy day does not allow the clothes to dry.

Practice Set 2

1. (*c*) We have five sense organs: eyes, ears, nose, tongue and skin. Brain is the thinking organ of our body. It is not a sense organ.

2. (*d*) Some rocks are very hard to break. They are called hard rocks. Granite, marble and sandstone are some examples of hard rocks.

3. (*b*) A–Goat gives us milk.

B–Hen gives us eggs.

C–Bees gives us bee wax to make candle. Sheep gives us wool

D–Which is used to make sweater.

4. (*c*) Posture is the position of our body while sitting, standing or walking. A good posture keeps us healthy and in good shape. It is neither a soft part our body nor a hard part of the body. It is also not the framework of bones.

5. (*c*)
I. The Sun gives us heat and **light**.
II. The half of the Earth that faces the Sun has **day**.
III. We have day and night because the **Earth** turns.
IV. Moon shines in the light of the **Sun**.

6. (*b*) Animals like deer, elephant, rhinoceros, giraffe, monkey and zebra eat only leaves, grass, green plants and fruits. These animals are called plant eating animals. Animals like tiger, bear, lion eat only flesh of other animals. These animals are called animal eating animals.

7. (*c*) We wear light cotton clothes on hot days as they keep our body cool.

We wear thick woollen clothes in winters as they keep our body warm. Raincoat is used during rainy season.

8. (*d*) The experiment shows that air has weight. When two balloons are placed on the rular they are equal. But, when one balloon gets pricked. The rular moves upward on the side where the balloon was deflated.

9. (*c*) We can keep the air fresh and clean by

(a) walking or using a bicycle instead of other vehicles that produce smoke.

(b) planting trees.

10. (*a*) We should not play with electricty. Playing with electricity can cause electric shock other methods which we should adopt are. Do not play with wire.

Wash the wet floors.

11. (*c*) The Earth have air and water. The Earth is also known as the blue planet.

Earth is the third planet of our solar system and life is possible on this planet.

12. (*b*) Big dipper is the shape of a large dipper with a handle. In India, this constellation is known as saptarishi mandal. The other constellations like scorpio, orion, ursa minor, etc. These can be easily located in the sky. There are 88 known constellations.

13. (*b*) (a) – Assam

(b) – Jammu and Kashmir

(c) – Punjab

(d) – West Bengal

14. (*c*) People build houses on stilts with sloping roofs in the areas where it rains heavily so that the rainwater can easily fall from the roofs.

15. (*a*) Good food habits help us to stay healthy and protect us from falling sick.

Good food habits are wash your hands with soap before and after eating every meal.

Eat freshly cooked food.

Eat your food at regular interval.

Printed by Libri Plureos GmbH in Hamburg,
Germany